Kate Clanchy is a writer, teacher and journalist. Her poetry collection *Slattern* won a Forward Prize. Her short story 'The Not-Dead and the Saved' won both the 2009 BBC National Short Story Award and the V. S. Pritchett Memorial Prize. Her novel *Meeting the English* was shortlisted for the Costa Prize.

Her BBC Radio 3 programme about her work with students was shortlisted for the Ted Hughes Prize. In 2018 she was appointed MBE for services to literature, and an anthology of her students' work, *England: Poems from a School*, was published to great acclaim. In 2019, she published *Some Kids I Taught and What They Taught Me*, a book about her experiences as a teacher; it won the Orwell Book Prize for Political Writing 2020.

She tweets as @KateClanchy1.

NOVELS

Meeting the English

POEMS

Slattern

Samarkand

Newborn

Selected Poems

The Picador Book of Birth Poems (ed.)

England: Poems from a School (ed.)

NON-FICTION

Antigona and Me

Some Kids I Taught and What They Taught Me

SHORT STORIES

The Not-Dead and the Saved

HOW TO GROW YOUR OWN POEM

Kate Clanchy

PICADOR

First published 2020 by Picador
an imprint of Pan Macmillan
The Smithson, 6 Briset Street, London ECIM 5NR
EU representative: Macmillan Publishers Ireland Limited,
Mallard Lodge, Lansdowne Village, Dublin 4
Associated companies throughout the world
www.panmacmillan.com

ISBN 978-1-5290-2469-2

3 5 7 9 8 6 4

A CIP catalogue record for this book is available from the British Library.

Typeset by Palimpsest Book Production Limited, Falkirk, Stirlingshire
Printed and bound by CPI Group (UK) Ltd, Croydon, CRO 4YY

Visit **www.picador.com** to read more about all our books
and to buy them. You will also find features, author interviews and
news of any author events, and you can sign up for e-newsletters
so that you're always first to hear about our new releases.

For my students, past, present and future.

Contents

x   How to Use this Book

Chapter 1
Getting Started

4   Put It All Down: A Place for Your Feelings: 'The Table'

11   Summoning Yourself: What Only You Know: 'Some People' and 'Things I Learned at University'

19   In General: Don't Try to Rhyme (right now)

21   The Way You See It (and no one else): 'A View of Things'

26   In General: If I Borrow a Shape is it Still My Own Poem?

28   Permission to Write: Join the Conversation

30   Room to Write: Make Room for Your Poems – and for Yourself

Chapter 2
Images

35   Image Generating: The Surrealists' Game

42   Sharpening Your Images: The Five Senses

47   Giving an Image Away: 'Sometimes Your Sadness Is'

48   In General: First Edits: Make Your Poem Fresher Not Grander

50   Little Movies: Extend Your Images

58   In General: Don't Hang Around with the Gerunds (they're just trying to glue up your poem)

62   In General: Titles

63   Home Movies

68   In General: How Far Can You Go?

70 Put Your Images through the Rinse Cycle:
    'A Guide to Love in Icelandic'

72 Move Right into Your Metaphor: Your Heart and My Heart

76   Permission to Write: Read Like a Poet

77   Room to Write: Room for Your Poems: Get Hold of Poetry

Chapter 3
Building Your Writing Process: Lists, Plots and Turns

80 Finding Your Writing Process

81 (Growing) Your Inner Checklist: The Furniture Game

87   In General: First Lines: No Time to Clear Your Throat

88 (Silhouette) Self-Portrait in a List: 'I Want the Confidence of'

91   In General: Leaving a Poem to Rise

94   In General: Last Lines: Keep Out of the Pulpit

95 Rhythmic Lists: 'Wasp'

97 A Turn for the Better: Build in a Volta

101 Oh! Lists of Three and Their Enduring Magic!

104   In General: Seeing Your Poem Freshly

105 The Heart: A List

108   In General: Are You Stuck but Know that There is More
            Poem to Write?

109   Permission to Write: Believe in Your Future and Your Past

111   Room to Write: Your Poetry Place, Your Poetry Palace

Chapter 4
Summoning Spells: Elegies, Letters,
Odes and Things that Get in the Way

114 I Don't Remember (except the images)

119   In General: How True is Your Truth?

120   Missing People 1: The Elegy

123   In General: Sounds that Tell You Something

124   Missing People 2: Ode to a Magical Object

128   In General: Does Your Poem Want to Be About
           Something (or Someone) Else?

129   Missing People 3: The Letter

133   In General: Poems Have Plots

137   In General: The Storyboard Test

139   Permission to Write: Defeating Your Inner Policeman

141   Room to Write: Private Space

Chapter 5
Finding Your Sound

145   Your Sound: 'I Come From'

151   In General: Finding Your Own Rhythm

153   Faster and Greener: Sounds of the Summer

157   In General: Where Your Rhythm Breaks

158   Finding Your Local Soundscape: 'On This Island'

164   In General: Punctuation: Poetry Percussion

165   Calling in Your People

169   Permission to Write: Sounding Right

171   Room to Write: Listen Out

Chapter 6
The White Space: Time Travel

174   Form and Shape: Time and Space

175   Writing Slo-Mo

177   Line Breaks and Breath

179   In General: Edge Words

180   Time Travel: The Stanza Break

183   In General: What Track is Your Poem Making?

184   (It's lonely here on) Couplet Island

189   Couplet Island 2

191   In General: Capital Letters

192   Time Travel Boxes: Regular Stanzas

196   In General: Find a Rule from Inside Your
               Poem

197   The Segue: Like This

202   More Practice: The 'Water' Challenge

204   The Ring Road: A Poem with No Stanzas

207   Permission to Write: Are You a Poet Yet?

209   Room to Write: Opening the Door

Chapter 7
Your Poem

214   Your Poem

223   List of Poem Titles

227   List of 'Permission to Write' Sections

229   List of 'Room to Write' Sections

231   List of 'In General' Sections

233   Acknowledgements

235   Permissions Acknowledgements

How to Use this Book

This is a practical book to help with what can easily seem an impractical, even frivolous problem: the yearning to write.

I wrote it because I take this longing very seriously. I believe that composing poetry is a fundamental human activity, like dance or singing, something we need to do and of which, even more than dance or music, we are deprived in the modern world. As a result, I believe there may be a lot of people with a poem-shaped hole in their lives. In fact, I'm sure there are, because so many people tell me so: not just the young people I teach, and their parents, friends and teachers, but all sorts of people of all ages, in all sorts of contexts. Some days I think it's everyone.

This book is practical because it is based on a teaching practice. I've been teaching people, old and young, to write poetry for more than twenty years. In that time, I have accumulated a number of techniques, exercises, pieces of advice and above all, poems, which I have found to actually work: by which I mean they consistently seem to help people write more fluently and confidently, more as themselves. The very best and most useful of them are assembled here.

I have sorted this material into sections so that we have separate segments at the end of chapters on the theoretical *Permission to Write* and the more tangible *Room to Write*. Bits of writing advice, meanwhile, have been attached to poems where they seemed particularly relevant, but also have their own headings so you can find them again for a different context. I've ordered the book so we begin with directed, supportive exercises and end with challenging, free-form ones. Inevitably, though – since writing poems is a multi-dimensional, holistic activity, and so is the process of helping someone with it – everything overlaps.

So, though this book will make sense if worked through from end to end, it can also be read forwards, backwards and sideways while making your own connections, much as a poem can. It can also be mined for teaching ideas, or enjoyed as an anthology of poems, or as a collection of thoughts about poetry. I hope, though, that most readers will use it practically, and get on with the writing.

Because when people tell me they want to write, I've found it best in practice not to linger on what is stopping them – that will always emerge later – but to show them a poem and invite them to answer it with one of their own. Your invitation is over the page.

1
GETTING STARTED

Writing a poem takes a lot of confidence. You have to believe that you and your experience belong in a poem, and are worth taking time over. Almost nobody finds that easy.

Here are four poems to get started with. Think of them as magic spells to build your sense of entitlement and permission.

'The Table' by Edip Cansever

'Some People' by Rita Ann Higgins

'What I Learned at University' by Kate Bingham

'A View of Things' by Edwin Morgan

All these poems work because they have strong rhetorical structures. You can borrow them, and, like scaffolding, they will hold your writing up.

Put It All Down:
A Place for Your Feelings: 'The Table'

Edip Cansever was a poet who also ran a carpet shop in the Grand Bazaar in Istanbul. He mixed his real, tangible trade with his intellectual life every day and believed that poems should also come from life and find their own forms. This beautiful, deceptively simple, poem is the fruit of that way of being.

This poem will not let you down. If you use its frame to hold your own experience you will create something beautiful.

Start by reading this poem several times, possibly out loud.

The Table

A man filled with the gladness of living
Put his keys on the table,
Put flowers in a copper bowl there.
He put his eggs and milk on the table.
He put there the light that came in through the window,
Sounds of a bicycle, sound of a spinning wheel.
The softness of bread and weather he put there.
On the table the man put
Things that happened in his mind.
What he wanted to do in life,
He put that there.
Those he loved, those he didn't love,
The man put them on the table too.
Three times three make nine:
The man put nine on the table.
He was next to the window next to the sky;
He reached out and placed on the table endlessness.
So many days he had wanted to drink a beer!
He put on the table the pouring of that beer.
He placed there his sleep and his wakefulness;
His hunger and his fullness he placed there.
Now that's what I call a table!
It didn't complain at all about the load.
It wobbled once or twice, then stood firm.
The man kept piling things on.

Edip Cansever, translated from the Turkish by Julia Clare Tillinghast
and Richard Tillinghast

Your Turn

Now you are going to write your own version. All you have to do is bring your own experience with you and be true to it. Nothing is too mundane for this poem – look how much Cansever gets out of a beer and some keys.

—

Start with someone coming home – a man, a woman, a boy.

It can be someone you know, or yourself, older or younger or right now. Even if it is you, though, use the third person (he or she or they) because that will give you a bit more distance and ease in the poem.

Who is coming home? How are they feeling?

A man full of . . .

A child full of . . .

Comes home.

—

Now you need a place to put things down – a sofa, a bed, a floor, a peg . . .

—

And puts his bag on the . . . it doesn't matter, but it does have to be a real place, or thing.

—

Now, he/she/they puts stuff down. They are concrete, tangible things. Things that are actually in the room:

keys . . . a phone . . .

She puts them down on the floor/bed/sofa . . .

—

Then he puts down some memories:

The sounds and touches and smells of the day . . .

What are they?

Make sure they are all real sensual things. Things that exist, that can be tasted or felt or smelt or heard but are not there in the room right now. The weather. The hum of the computer. The sound of the stairwell. There might be some memories from further back, too, but make sure they are all concrete and clear.

—

Now he can put down some things that 'happened in his mind'.

Things that aren't in the room, or that happened that day but are floating in the memory nevertheless.

A wish.

A sum.

A formula.

A recipe or instruction.

A line of poetry or a phrase from a song.

Someone's name.

A worry.

A person – someone the protaganist loves or hates, what they said.

Your poem is getting quite long now, and the pile of stuff is getting big.

The pile is made of:

Things in the hand,

Remembered things,

Things of the mind.

—

But you can pile on more.

If you like, you can go for something bigger, more abstract – pain, or longing, or death – after all, Cansever has 'endlessness'.

But balance it with something small and concrete (the longing for a beer), and make sure it goes down safely on your peg or table.

One more big thing . . . maybe just one more . . .

Something you've always wanted –

—

But this pile is getting big.

Let's go back to the concrete: the table/peg/sofa.

What is it doing under all this weight?

—

Talk to it. Congratulate it. Thank it. Show it to the reader.

It's doing well.

—

So are you.

You have a poem.

—

Read it through.

Type it out.

Keep it safe.

A couple of encouraging examples. These are both 'table' poems. Michael dashed his off in twenty minutes, as usual.

The Never-Ending Pile

An old lady filled with the satisfaction of living
Put her walking stick on the table,
and stood up young and strong.
She put her jacket covered with snow on the table
She put her shopping trolley on there too.
On there she put the voice of her dead husband.
On there she put the mole she had cut off.
On that table, her first kiss and her last,
The one bitchy friend,
And the one she had tea with, an hour ago.
Tick, tock, tick, tock, the sound of the clock –
She put that on the table.
Reaching up through the sky
She grabbed the moon
And smiled at Armstrong
And put that on the table.
And her wish for wealth and freedom
And for grace and for quickening the pace of world peace,
And her future, a tombstone,
All on the table.

A crackle here, a crackle there
But the table stood like her, young and strong.
Her never-ending pile grew.

Michael Egbe (sixteen)

Mohamed was a young
refugee from Syria, just
beginning to learn
English.

Bin

When I go back home
I throw all my stuff on the floor:
my bag, my jumper, my trousers, my shoes,
my tie and my tee-shirt; my feelings,
my memories, the smells of life
all on the floor.
I put 2x2 and my 4 ideas
on the table;
the stupid words I learned from my friends,
in the bin.
I think about playing football,
and when I will play more,
and I put this thought
under my pillow,
because I need to keep it with me.

Hey bin, you've got
all those stupid English words in you.

Mohamed Assaf (twelve)

Summoning Yourself:

What Only You Know: 'Some People' and 'Things I Learned at University'

When you look at your 'table' poem, you will probably notice one or two little details that somehow seem to work. In Mohamed's poem, it's the football dream that has to be kept under the pillow; in Michael Egbe's, probably the miniature Armstrong the old lady plucks from the moon. Those are the details that unexpectedly move us, the ones we are willing to trust, the ones that just seem true: the authentic details.

Authenticity is something we all recognize and admire in other people's writing, but not necessarily something beginning writers appreciate in their own work, not because they are stupid, but because they lack confidence. It's very easy to think that your own experience doesn't belong in a poem because, well, it happened to you, and you're not a poet, are you?

But if you are going to create a sense of authenticity in your own poems, you will have to draw on your own life. This doesn't mean only writing down things that actually happened, or exposing your diary entries to the world – many of the truest-seeming things, paradoxically, are partly made up – but it does mean visiting your lived experience for precise observations and telling details.

To do that, you have to believe that your life belongs in a poem – and that's where these next two poems come in. Writing versions of these poems can help because they provide strong rhetorical frames for your experience – shapes. Glimpsing your life in this frame, like seeing yourself in a beautiful photograph, will help you view your experience freshly and value it more.

Do you sometimes feel
that your life experience
just isn't written down in
poems? That you only
know un-literary things?

So did Rita Ann Higgins,
who grew up as one of
thirteen children in a
close family in working-
class Galway in the
sixties. (The 'Vincent de
Paul man' dispensed
charity.)

Some People

Some people know what it is like
to be called a cunt in front of their children
to be short for the rent
to be short for the light
to be short for school books
to wait in Community Welfare waiting rooms full of smoke
to wait two years to have a tooth looked at
to wait another two years to have a tooth out (the same tooth)
to be half strangled by your varicose veins, but you're 198th on the
    list
to talk into a banana on a jobsearch scheme
to talk into a banana on a jobsearch dream
to be out of work
to be out of money
to be out of fashion
to be out of friends
to be in for the Vincent de Paul man
(sorry, mammy isn't in today she's gone to Mars for the weekend)
to be in Puerto Rico for the blanket man
to be dead for the coal man
(sorry, mammy passed away in her sleep, overdose of coal in the
    teapot)
to be in hospital unconscious for the rent man (St Jude's ward 4th
    floor)
to be second hand
to be second class
to be no class

to be looked down on
to be pissed on
to be shat on

and other people don't.

Rita Ann Higgins

Your Turn

If this poem speaks to you, try your own version.

It is a powerful poem for releasing anger, so start your own poem by thinking of an experience you have that most people around you ignore.

To be poor, for example,

to be of colour,

to come from a 'different' family of some kind,

to have illness in your family,

to have experienced a miscarriage, or a death . . .

Now,

Borrow the structure directly. Fill it in with concrete details from your own experience.

Your first line is *Some people know*

Or *Some women know*

Or *Some kids know* . . . or

There are those who understand,

or *There are those who have seen* . . .

Then make lists from your experience using 'to'.

To be called . . .

To be short of . . .

To wait

To wait.

To be out of

To long for

To wish for

To never

—

End with a bang. Higgins is very clever with this – she puts only the general statements, 'to be second class/to be looked down on', right at the end of her poem. Everything up till then is made of (often funny) particular, concrete statements. This keeps her powder dry. Do the same with yours.

End your poem:

And some people don't

And there are those who don't

Or . . . something else that you came up with . . .

You have a poem!

There are lots of ways of diminishing your own experience and excluding it (and you) from poetry. Feeling that you are too poor or too foreign is one of them. Feeling that your life is too middle class and privileged is another. This witty and truthful poem boldly ignores that anxiety.

Things I Learned at University

How to bike on cobblestones and where to signal right.
How to walk through doors held by Old Etonians
and not scowl. How to make myself invisible in seminars
by staring at the table. How to tell Victorian Gothic from Medieval.
How to eat a Mars bar in the Bodleian. When to agree
with everything in theory. How to cultivate a taste for sherry.

Where to bike on the pavement after dark. How to sabotage a hunt.
When to sunbathe topless in the Deer Park. When to punt.
How to hitch a lift and when to walk and where to run.
When not to address my tutors formally. How to laugh at Latin
    puns
and when to keep quiet and preserve my integrity.
How to celebrate an essay crisis. When to sleep through fire
    alarms.

How to bike no-handed, how to slip a condom on with one.
When to smoke a joint and when to swig champagne.
When to pool a tip and how to pull a pint. A bit of history.
When to listen to friends and whether to take them seriously.
At the same time how to scorn tradition and enjoy it.
How to live like a king, quite happily, in debt.

Kate Bingham

Your Turn

If this poem seems to chime with you more strongly than the Rita Ann Higgins poem, try a version of it instead.

Down the left-hand margin of a piece of paper, write

Five 'How to's

Five 'When to's and

Five 'Where to's.

Then think of a time in your life which changed you, for better or worse, and give yourself a heading:

Things I Learned . . . (at Nursery, Primary School, University, in France, in Bed, at the Sea, at Summer Camp).

Then, working quickly and not too critically, fill in your list.

Finish with a slightly different line: *And never to . . . And not to forget.*

Just to demonstrate that the same frame can contain very different experiences, here is Michael Egbe's response to Kate Bingham – the same Michael who wrote 'The Never-Ending Pile'. He was nearly at the end of his time at school when he wrote this, and it was one of the last poems he created in one of my workshops. I'd known him for four years by then, and this was the first time he'd ever mentioned the year he spent at military school in Nigeria when he was fourteen.

Things I Learned at Military School

How to wake at 4.00am
to roll on wet grass
to run a thousand miles.
The smell of gunpowder,
the brass chill of a bullet.
I know the chant of war songs,
the thump of angry feet
in a march, their dusty tracks,
and how to lie face down
and still under
a hundred lashes. I know
the bruises. I know
how to mount a rifle,
how to look through the scope.
How easy it is to squeeze
the trigger. To wait and listen
for the recoil. But not much
about peace. It seemed
to be something
we couldn't afford.

Michael Egbe (eighteen)

In General: Don't Try to Rhyme (right now)

Try writing these first poems without rhyme.

I'm not giving this advice because I don't like rhyme, or don't use it myself, or because it's not fashionable: I love rhyme, always use it (there is plenty in my poem 'Patagonia', for example, though it's not at the end of the lines) and it's always in fashion.

But it's too easy, when you are a beginning poet and want to make your thoughts sound like a poem, to turn to the first and most familiar form of poetry you learned when you were young – full rhyming couplets. And while one rhyming couplet is easy to produce – 'Double, double, toil and trouble/Fire burn and cauldron bubble' – two or three are not. Once you are hunting for a rhyme, you also tend to start thinking of an end to your sentence and to your thought, and so the rhyme starts to write the poem for you. You don't want that: you are writing your *own* poem.

Even rhyming every second line can be hard. Full rhymes – 'hard' with 'yard', for example – are rare in English, much rarer than, for instance, in Italian, where huge numbers of nouns end in the same masculine or feminine 'o's and 'a's. This affects the way we write in English, especially at length. Dante's *Divine Comedy*, Italy's classic text, is 14,233 lines of *terza rima*, which has an intricate pattern of end rhymes. *Terza rima* is fiendishly difficult in English because of our paucity of rhyme, so Dante is often translated into our classic English metre, Shakespearean blank verse, which has rhythm but no rhymes at all. Blank verse, in fact, five beats in a line, is very often what beginning poets most readily produce in English, though they may not lay it out with the matching line breaks. It's certainly a more natural, open mode to aim for than rhyming couplets.

Another thing: because they are rare, rhymes in English are *loud*. We notice them. They often make us laugh. This is great in comic verse, or in song lyrics, where you need the emphasis, but they can boom out of a gentle poem like a full hand on the kettle drum. Of course, this can in itself be fabulous. But, when you are starting out, it's often easier to hear the other notes of your range if you don't aim for full rhyme. This doesn't mean your poem will be flat: you will almost certainly find yourself using half-rhyme and assonance (vowel rhyme) all over the place. Listen out for them – those are your own sounds.

The Way You See It (and no one else):
'A View of Things'

In this poem Edwin Morgan shows us his view of things, exactly how he saw his world, through a series of concrete details. He tells us what he likes to eat and how different phrases fire off strings of associations in his mind. He uses very personal associations – *what I love about Mabel is her teeter* – but somehow manages to communicate to all of us.

(Notes: Bratach Gorm is a mountain. In the olden days, as some of you may remember, newspapers had misprints, hence 'etaoin shrdl'. The 'setae' of a hog is its whiskers, though I think Morgan wants you to look that one up. An 'ion engine' is one that feeds on its own energy, hence going on

A View of Things

what I love about dormice is their size
what I hate about rain is its sneer
what I love about the Bratach Gorm is its unflappability
what I hate about scent is its smell
what I love about newspapers is their etaoin shrdl
what I hate about philosophy is its pursed lip
what I love about Rory is his old grouse
what I hate about Pam is her pinkie
what I love about semi-precious stones is their preciousness
what I hate about diamonds is their mink
what I love about poetry is its ion engine
what I hate about hogs is their setae
what I love about love is its porridge-spoon
what I hate about hate is its eyes
what I love about hate is its salts
what I hate about love is its dog
what I love about Hank is his string vest
what I hate about the twins is their three gloves
what I love about Mabel is her teeter
what I hate about gooseberries is their look, feel, smell and taste
what I love about the world is its shape
what I hate about a gun is its lock, stock and barrel
what I love about bacon-and-eggs is its predictability
what I hate about derelict buildings is their reluctance to
  disintegrate

for ever, and is used on rockets going into deep space. The poet is wrong about gooseberries.)

How do you remember your childhood home? By an abstract label – 'safety', 'contentment' – or by the smell of the warm wood at the back of the airing cupboard?

What is the essence of a person for you? Their name? Or the cut of a jacket, a curl of hair, the wobble of a heel? Would you put that in a poem? Why not, when it works so well for Morgan, when, the 'further out' the description, the nearer it seems to come?

what I love about a cloud is its unpredictability
what I hate about you, chum, is your china
what I love about many waters is their inability to quench love

Edwin Morgan

Your Turn

Use Edwin Morgan's poem as an 'ion engine'.

Copy his form.

Write down the left-hand margin of the page:

What I love about

What I hate about

What I love about

What I hate about . . .

—

Then fill it in. Work quickly, letting your mind move freely, making sure that all your details are real and concrete and come from your own experience.

What I love about – a food

What I hate about – an animal

What I love about – a kind of weather

What I hate about – a country

What I love about – a city

What I hate about – a landmark

What I love about – a person

What I hate about – a different person

—

Now you can move on to some abstract concepts.

What I hate about love is . . .

What I love about resentment is . . .

You could use any feelings you like . . . love, kindness, *Schadenfreude*, relief . . .

But make sure you stay concrete in your responses. You can't make us see or smell or touch an abstraction by using another abstraction.

What I love about love is its kindness is boring

What I love about love is its porridge-spoon is great.

—

Land your poems somewhere big at the end – Morgan uses 'many waters'.

Han Sun uses maths.

No Maths Involved

What I love about winter is the big cup of cocoa
What I hate about winter is the numb fingers
What I hate about movies is the clichés
What I love about books is their world
What I love about cats is their cuteness
What I hate about Marmite is the sickening smell
What I love about people is their freedom and generosity
What I hate about people is when they have none
What I hate about the world is the lack of equality
What I hate about politics is everything
What I love about long drives is stopping off for coffee
What I hate about love is that it is undeniable
What I love about love is that there is no maths involved

Han Sun Nkumu (sixteen)

Where will you land?

In General: If I Borrow a Shape is it Still My Own Poem?

Yes. All poems lean on or start from other poems, and some of the most profound and brilliant do so in obvious ways.

Jen Hadfield's poem (next) is her own, though it uses a form which Edwin Morgan invented. Despite borrowing from Morgan, it doesn't take anything away from him. In fact, it gives back to him, because poetry, as he pointed out, is an ion engine, endlessly recycling its own energy.

You can be part of that engine. If you finish a poem in the 'What I love about' shape it will belong to you, but also to Morgan and Hadfield. If you publish the poem, you can acknowledge that by using the courtesy form 'after' under your title: e.g. 'after Edwin Morgan and Jen Hadfield'.

As you write more, you may well find yourself writing poems which you know began by leaning on the shape of a particular other poem but which is now so different that readers would not recognize the connection. Then it's your choice whether or not to use 'after' in the title. Jen Hadfield chose not to write 'after Edwin Morgan' in her poem, but she acknowledged him in the title, which refers to the line 'what I hate about love is its dog' in 'A View of Things'.

Love's Dog

What I love about love is its diagnosis
What I hate about love is its prognosis

What I hate about love is its me me me
What I love about love is its Eat-me/Drink-me

What I love about love is its petting zoo
What I love about love is its zookeeper – you

What I love about love is its truth serum
What I hate about love is its shrinking potion

What I love about love is its doubloons
What I love about love is its bird-bones

What I hate about love is its boil-wash
What I love about love is its spin-cycle

What I loathe about love is its burnt toast and bonemeal
What I hate about love is its bent cigarette

What I love about love is its pirate
What I hate about love is its sick parrot

Jen Hadfield

Join the Conversation

'Of all the art forms, poetry is the most economical. It is the one which is the most secret, which requires the least physical labour, the least material, and the one which can be done between shifts, in the hospital pantry, on the subway, and on scraps of surplus paper.'

So said the great American poet and essayist Audre Lorde, contrasting poetry with novel writing. She should be right – yet most beginning writers still start on novels. Despite being so accessible, poetry has a difficult reputation. It is seen as more elevated than prose, and harder. Poets are often thought of as special people, eccentric, super talented, and marked from birth. It's all very intimidating.

If you feel stymied by these ideas, or by the anxiety that your thoughts are not original enough or your experiences not spiritual enough to belong in a poem, here is a thought. For most people over most of time, poetry hasn't consisted of single poems by named (male, white, dead) poets in books. Mostly, poetry has consisted of stories and chants handed down and exchanged among working people going about their daily lives. Mostly, poetry hasn't had a single author, or been written down, but has been recited, sung, shared, adapted and passed on as seemed useful. And, though all societies have a special place for talented poets, most people over most time would at some point in their lives have made up a few lines of poetry, in the same way that they would have added a note to a work song, or danced a new step at a wedding. Those lines would probably have been in answer to someone else's lines – the way rap artists still riff off one another. Poetry, in short, until very recently, was a varied, noisy, general conversation, not a silent solo art form.

It's easier to join in a conversation than it is to make a speech, just as it is easier to open your mouth to sing if you are in a choir, or to dance in a group. Most art forms support beginners by sharing. No one expects a prima ballerina or opera diva to train entirely alone and walk fully formed on the stage – but we do have those expectations of poetry. If you can put those expectations aside, you may well feel more free to write.

Rather than setting out to be 'a poet', try allowing yourself to join in the poetry conversation. We all retain that ancient capacity to answer a poem with another one: it's much easier and more natural than writing an essay about a poem. All you have to do is let yourself read a poem and allow answering thoughts to form in your mind. The news is: a writer is a person who writes, and a poet is someone writing a poem – you.

Make Room for Your Poems – and for Yourself

As Audre Lorde says, poetry can happen anywhere. But it helps to have:

A Place. Set aside a writing place. A particular chair with your laptop or corner of your desk will do, so long as you feel secure there.

A Time. Make yourself a writing date and mark it in your diary, whether it's a half-hour first thing in the morning, or a Saturday afternoon.

A Folder. Value your poems in a tangible way: have a special folder or notebook for your work, or at the very least a special file on your computer.

If you keep waiting for inspiration, the time for writing won't arrive. If you give yourself a time to join in the poetry conversation, a place to do so, permission and a prompt to answer, your poem will come too.

2 IMAGES

No ideas but in things: William Carlos Williams

Poems are many different shapes, but all poems are figurative. That is, they use images – similes or metaphors – to connect things with other things and to make a memorable picture.

Everyone uses images in everyday speech too. We shout metaphors in insult and wit, exploit them to explain statistics or get elected, embed them into our languages in cliché, utilize them daily in a thousand ways, so it is perhaps a little strange that the ability to create them is not one we explicitly cherish or cultivate in language education. As a teacher, I've observed that most five-year-olds can effortlessly create an image for a shining haiku, but that many sixth-formers, especially the most academic, will turn in a cliché instead because their ability to associate idea and thing in an original way has never been given any exercise or credit. You too may well have buried your image-making capacity as you went through the education system, especially if you are very clever, and wanted to oblige. This chapter focuses on digging up that rusty ability, knocking off the clay and polishing it up to a shine.

Image Generating:
The Surrealists' Game

When I work with groups, I almost always play a game which
helps to reconnect people to their image-making ability. I did not
invent this game: I was taught it by the poet Carol Ann Duffy. She
did not invent it either, though. In fact, it is rumoured to have been
invented by the Surrealist painter Salvador Dalí and his group, and
to have been played over espresso and absinthe in the Spanish
desert in order to work up some new ideas. It probably is best in a
group or pair, but you can also play it on your own: rational self
against inner five-year-old, calling up your subconscious as if with
a Ouija board. If you are on your own, you'll have to be extra
serious about it. Absinthe is optional, but if you are going to do
this, set aside an hour, and follow the exercise through carefully.

You'll need some paper, either small notelets or A4 torn into
quarters, and you'll need at least sixteen of them. Make them into a
nice little pile. Find a pen.

Remember the difference between an *abstract* and a *concrete* noun.

Concrete nouns can be found by the senses. Remember all five of
yours: sight, touch, taste, smell, hearing. Five wise monkeys. Eyes,
fingers, mouth, nose, ears.

Abstract nouns can't be sensed. They are ideas – *racism* or *fame* – or
feelings – *doubt* or *hope*.

Think of an abstract noun – *hope* – and write it on your first piece
of paper.

On the second piece of paper, pretend briefly to be the dictionary,
the definition of that noun – *a faith or wish that circumstances will
improve in the future.*

Now do the same with a concrete noun, and your third piece of paper, e.g. *bird*.

On the fourth bit of paper – the definition of that noun – *vertebrate with feathers. Descended from dinosaurs.*

Now repeat: abstract noun, definition, concrete noun, definition, and again, nouns and definitions on separate bits of paper.

You will need at least eight nouns and definitions.

When you have enough, gather the nouns in one pile, and the definitions in another, and shuffle both.

Now take the first noun off the top of its pile, and match with the first definition.

Hope is a vertebrate with feathers. Descended from dinosaurs.

Bird is a faith or wish that circumstances will improve in the future.

Was Emily Dickinson
playing the Surrealists'
Game?

It seems possible.

Hope

Hope is the thing with feathers –
That perches in the soul –
And sings the tune without the words –
And never stops – at all –

And sweetest – in the Gale – is heard –
And sore must be the storm –
That could abash the little Bird
That kept so many warm –

I've heard it in the chillest land –
And on the strangest Sea –
Yet – never – in Extremity,
It asked a crumb – of me.

Emily Dickinson

Fame

Fame is a bee.
It has a song—
It has a sting—
Ah, too, it has a wing.

Emily Dickinson

Rachel really was playing the Surrealists' Game during one of my classes. She started with 'Want' matching with the definition of 'snake'. Then she made over Want into a person.

Want

Want is quiet but it sticks around.
It takes a seat before it makes itself known.
Want's eyes glint, and its tongue flickers.
Want will listen, and wait, and study,
it learns everything. It learns you.

Want smiles and soon after it laughs –
not with you.
Want mocks in whispers and sometimes
(if you are unlucky)
Want will shout.

Rachel Gittens (sixteen)

Langston Hughes, one of the founding figures of Black American literature, also shows how a surreal analogy – in this case ripening fruit – can be political and powerful. He's writing about Harlem in the 1930s, when the hope of Black Americans in the first decades of the twentieth century were being destroyed. It's all about the senses: textures, smells, tastes.

Harlem

What happens to a dream deferred?

    Does it dry up
like a raisin in the sun?
Or fester like a sore—
And then run?
Does it stink like rotten meat?
Or crust and sugar over—
like a syrupy sweet?

    Maybe it just sags
like a heavy load.

    Or does it explode?

Langston Hughes

Your Turn

Try a poem.

Write down an abstraction that interests you: desire, or *Schadenfreude*, or Brexit. You can use a place or time like 'Harlem' if you like. Now, use a concrete metaphor to define it.

So maybe your poem makes an abstraction into:

a person (like Rachel Gittens)

or a creature (like Emily Dickinson).

Or something else,

even a food (like Langston Hughes).

But your poem makes an *idea* into a *thing*.

Your poem is short.

It doesn't rhyme.

It isn't a haiku.

It isn't an acrostic.

It's just you,

making an abstract idea concrete,

expressing an association that's real for you.

Trusting that it will be real for other people.

Surprise yourself.

Write it down.

Sharpening Your Images:
The Five Senses

As you write and rewrite, it helps to have an inner store of questions you always ask of your own writing.

A good one is: does my writing appeal to the senses?

Remember all five of them:
Smell
Taste
Hearing
Touch
Sight

Five wise monkeys. Eyes, fingers, mouth, nose, ears.

All of the senses are in this Carol Ann Duffy poem – they are what makes it alive.

Hard to Say

I asked him to give me an image for Love, something I could see,
or imagine seeing, or something that, because of the word,
for its smell, would make me remember, something possible
to hear. *Don't just say Love*, I said, *Love, love, I love you.*

On the way back, I thought of our love, and how, lately,
I too have grown lazy in expressing it, snuggling up to you
in bed, idly murmuring those tired clichés without even thinking.
My words have been grubby confetti, faded, tacky, blown far

from the wedding feast. And so it was with a sudden shock of love,
like a peacock flashing wide its hundred eyes, or a boy's voice
flinging top G to the roof of an empty church, or a bottle
of French perfume knocked off the shelf, spilling into the steamy
    bath

I wanted you. After the wine, the flowers I brought you drowned
in the darkening light. As we slept, we breathed their scent all
    night.

Carol Ann Duffy

Your Turn

Lean on Carol Ann Duffy's poem to make your own.

If you like, play another round of the Surrealists' Game.

Think of an abstraction – nationalism, capitalism, philosophy – or an emotion – love, sadness, loss – that you'd like to write about.

That abstraction is your title. Carol Ann Duffy has 'Love'.

Now, go through the senses.

What does this abstraction smell of, to you?

Love smells of:

a bottle

of French perfume knocked off the shelf, spilling into the steamy bath

—

What does love taste of?

the wine

Trust your personal associations. Build them up on the page. You are allowed more than one answer. If you find the answers a little embarrassing – if they make the hairs on the back of your neck lift – then definitely write them down.

What does love sound like?

a boy's voice

flinging top G to the roof of an empty church

What does love feel like?

we breathed their scent all night.

What does it look like?

like a peacock flashing wide its hundred eyes

Linnet followed this exercise to start her poem about hope.

Linnet uses the word she was defining, hope, at the end of each stanza, not the beginning, and she gets firmer and surer in her definitions as she moves through – from 'like hope' to 'that's hope' to 'Hope'. It's a simple trick but very effective. Try it, or, even more simply, use your original word only once, at the very end of your poem.

Hope

When you can count stars behind clouds
and read tea leaves in a teabag;
that's like hope.

Watering plants in the rain; tuning
a harp and tuning it back again:
that's hope.

Breathing life into glass on the back seat
of a bus; staying on till it clears;
writing poems on Mondays;
kneading bread out of air:
Hope.

Linnet Drury (fifteen)

This is my version of that
exercise, written when I
was twenty-seven and
directly in response to the
Carol Ann Duffy poem. I
really was going out with
a man with no sense of
smell. He dumped me
shortly afterwards and
now I have forgotten his
second name. The poem,
on the other hand, has
done rather well, proving
that poetry is magic.

Poem for a Man with No Sense of Smell

This is simply to inform you:

that the thickest line in the kink of my hand
smells like the feel of an old school desk,
the deep carved names worn sleek with sweat;

that beneath the spray of my expensive scent
my armpits sound a bass note strong
as the boom of a palm on a kettle drum;

that the wet flush of my fear is sharp
as the taste of an iron pipe, midwinter,
on a child's hot tongue; and that sometimes,

in a breeze, the delicate hairs on the nape
of my neck, just where you might bend
your head, might hesitate and brush your lips,

hold a scent frail and precise as a fleet
of tiny origami ships, just setting out to sea.

Kate Clanchy

Giving an Image Away:
'Sometimes Your Sadness Is'

What are the images you get from other people? How do you see their feelings?

This poem gets its energy from giving the abstract feeling to someone else, a lover. The poet and the lover together are grappling with the sadness, trying to describe it and define it. Their sadness is the sound of the neighbours having a party; feels like a rock stuck in the lawnmower, looks like a yacht going by . . .

Sometimes your sadness is a yacht

huge, white and expensive, like an anvil
dropped from heaven: how will we get onboard,
up there, when it hurts our necks to look?

Other times it is a rock on the lawn, and matter
can never be destroyed. But today we hold it
to the edge of our bed, shutting our eyes

on another opened hour and listening
to our neighbours' voices having the voices
of their friends around for lunch.

Jack Underwood

Try a poem like this.
Think of a person, your *you*.
Think of one of their qualities: happiness/silence/neediness.
Think of some images for that quality. Use your five senses.
Begin your poem.
Sometimes your neediness is . . .

In General: First Edits: Make Your Poem Fresher Not Grander

Editing poems is scary – often scarier than writing them, because you actually have to read your own words! You might even feel tempted to throw away the draft instead – many people do. Don't! If you are even tempted, put your poem to one side, and make an appointment with yourself in a week or a month to have another look.

When you are ready to edit again, read your poem over. You need to get a fresh perspective on it – a simple way of doing this is to read it aloud. How does it sound? What are the best bits? Does anything make you blush, or cry?

Remember that you want your poem to sound like you, not like 'a poem' and definitely not like 'a beginning poem'. So have a careful think about the details you have used: do they connect to your experience? Can you see them, hear them, feel them? Do they spark off memories? Are they authentic? If they aren't, take them out, and add in a few that are. Now, try a little general weeding – the following tricks make most poems clearer and brighter:

Take out the abstract adjectives, especially if they are describing an abstract thing. An 'immense innocence' is not helping your poem to be clear, even if it sounds nice. In fact, question all your adjectives – ask each one if it is really helping, and throw it away if it is not. (Helping with sound does count as helping.)

Take out the adverbs – 'usually', 'enormously', 'hastily' – your verbs will almost always seem stronger on their own.

Take out the intensifiers. No one needs 'very', and definitely not 'somewhat'.

Tell yourself that you don't have to boss the audience about with adverbs and adjectives and intensifiers. We'll get it.

Believe in your own writing.

Believe in your own experience.

Believe in your own poem.

Little Movies:
Extend Your Images

This is another poem based, like Carol Ann Duffy's or Jack Underwood's, on the definition of an abstraction through metaphors, but here, each metaphor is extended. The images have been allowed to grow into a scene, and filled out with details: the 'single-engine' plane, the 'grassy' landing strip. It's filmic – we understand it from cartoons we have seen or movies we have watched more than from our actual experience – and so it has a surreal, almost comical quality. But that doesn't stop it being intimate or memorable – after all, our collective subconscious is full of film these days.

Happiness

There's just no accounting for happiness,
or the way it turns up like a prodigal
who comes back to the dust at your feet
having squandered a fortune far away.

And how can you not forgive?
You make a feast in honour of what
was lost, and take from its place the finest
garment, which you saved for an occasion
you could not imagine, and you weep night and day
to know that you were not abandoned,
that happiness saved its most extreme form
for you alone.

No, happiness is the uncle you never
knew about, who flies a single-engine plane
onto the grassy landing strip, hitchhikes
into town, and inquires at every door
until he finds you asleep midafternoon
as you so often are during the unmerciful
hours of your despair.

It comes to the monk in his cell.
It comes to the woman sweeping the street
with a birch broom, to the child
whose mother has passed out from drink.
It comes to the lover, to the dog chewing

a sock, to the pusher, to the basketmaker,
and to the clerk stacking cans of carrots
in the night.
    It even comes to the boulder
in the perpetual shade of pine barrens,
to rain falling on the open sea,
to the wineglass, weary of holding wine.

Jane Kenyon

Jane Kenyon wrote her poem in the 1990s. This next poem, by
the New Zealand poet Hera Lindsay Bird, comes from the
internet age and is filled not so much with film references as
internet gifs, such as–

*Love like the recurring decimal of some huge, indivisible number
or a well thrown boomerang
coming to rest in the soft curve of your hand*

which almost makes you think of a very well-put-together
advertisement.

Both poems, though, are *animated*: as you read through them both,
notice how much action there is, starting with the abstraction itself.
Happiness and Love are moving through these pages like the hero
of the movie, flying and enquiring and above all, coming back.

Love Comes Back

Like your father,
twenty years later with the packet of cigarettes he went out for
Like Monday but this is the nineteenth century
& you're a monied aristocrat with no conception of the working
    week

Like a haunted board game
pried from the rubble of an archaeological dig site
You roll the dice & bats come flooding out your heart
like molten grappling hooks
your resolve weakening . . .
like the cord of an antique disco ball . . .

Love like the recurring decimal of some huge, indivisible number
or a well thrown boomerang
coming to rest in the soft curve of your hand

Love comes back . . .
like a murderer returning to the scene of the crime . . .
or not returning . . .
yet still the crime remains . . .
like love . . .
observed or unobserved . . .
written in blood on the walls of some ancient civilisation
in an idiom so old
we have no contemporary vernacular equivalent

Love like Windows 95
The greatest, most user-friendly Windows of them all
Those four little panes of light
Like the stained glass of an ancient church
vibrating in the sunlit rubble
of the twentieth century

Your face comes floating up in my crystal ball . . .

The lights come on at the bottom of the ocean
& here we are alone again . . .

Late November
we ride the black escalator of the mountain
& emerge into the altitude of our last year
The rabbit in the grass gives us something wild to aim for
It twists into spring like a living bell

I have to be here always telling you that
no matter how far I travel beyond you
love will stay tethered
like an evil kite I want to always reel back in
As if we could just turn and wade back
through the ghost of some ancient season
or wake each morning in the heat of a vanished life

Love comes back
from where it's never gone . . . It was here the whole time

like a genetic anomaly waiting to reveal itself
Like spring at the museum, after centuries of silence
the bronze wings of gladiator helmets trembling in their
    sockets . . .
Grecian urns sprouting new leaves . . .

Love like a hand from the grave
trembling up into the sunlight of the credit sequence
the names of the dead
pouring down the screen
like cool spring rain

Hera Lindsay Bird

Your Turn

Write a 'little movie' poem

Spend some time reading both 'Happiness' and 'Love Comes Back'.

—

Let the images form fully in your mind. Play them behind your eyes like little movies. You could even draw them if you are talented that way, or just imagine a film to accompany them.

—

Now carry that visual way of thinking into a poem of your own.

—

Choose an abstraction. You can play another round of the Surrealists' Game for inspiration, or you could simply name a feeling that is close to you right now.

—

This is going to be an animated poem, so make sure your abstraction has a verb attached. You can borrow 'comes back' if you like. But 'returns', 'makes itself known', 'cuts in', 'shines', 'bears down', 'weighs in', 'dances', 'walks on' will all work.

—

Now, imagine as many moving images for your abstraction as you can, and write them down in plenty of detail.

—

Remember to be the movie director, using light and shade, and always making sure the reader has someone to follow.

—

For a final stanza, borrow Jane Kenyon's technique of using repeated phrases and shorter and shorter examples – *it comes to . . . it comes to . . . it comes to.*

Each stanza in Aisha's
poem is a little scene.
Each has a verb. The
images are very diverse,
but the poem has
coherence and
excitement.

Grief

When the computer shoots the printer
and deletes the whole folder
we write grief.

When the death has already happened
yet your great grandma still sits in her chair,
that is grief.

When words twist into one another creating a song
that explodes in your eyes,
that's grief.

And in the blackberry bushes where we hid
our love for one another,
grief also sits

holding a sphere and wearing a crown of thorns,
letting the blood roll over his torn head.
Grief is also

in the hospice next to your cousin, knitting
a hat for her moon head, and when
she dies grief sleeps

under your aunt's bed.

Aisha Borja (sixteen)

In General: Don't Hang Around with the Gerunds (they're just trying to glue up your poem)

Gerunds are verbs used as nouns, and in English they have 'ing' on the end: swimming, walking, seeing, hearing . . .

Poets are very drawn to them. They do nice poetic things. They still the action. They suit a contemplative turn of mind. They rhyme (with each other). They give you an iambic (ta-tum) beat. But they can also have a cloying, clogging effect.

No, happiness is the uncle you never
knew about, flying a single-engine plane
onto the grassy landing strip, hitchhiking
into town, inquiring at every door
finding you asleep mid afternoon

is a degree less clear and animated than

No, happiness is the uncle you never
knew about, who flies a single-engine plane
onto the grassy landing strip, hitchhikes
into town, and inquires at every door
until he finds you asleep mid-afternoon

for instance.

And 'love coming back' is definitely less good than 'love comes back'.

Aisha's poem above has very few gerunds, and where they are used, they are doing a different job to the active verbs.

Check your poem for gerunds. Try an active verb instead.

A Little Nature Movie

There's a miniature nature documentary in the centre of this poem – the miracle of a grasshopper, in all its intricacy, eating some sugar. Read it through and start thinking of your own poem.

The Summer Day

Who made the world?
Who made the swan, and the black bear?
Who made the grasshopper?
This grasshopper, I mean–
the one who has flung herself out of the grass,
the one who is eating sugar out of my hand,
who is moving her jaws back and forth instead of up and down–
who is gazing around with her enormous and complicated eyes.
Now she lifts her pale forearms and thoroughly washes her face.
Now she snaps her wings open, and floats away.
I don't know exactly what a prayer is.
I do know how to pay attention, how to fall down
into the grass, how to kneel down in the grass,
how to be idle and blessed, how to stroll through the fields,
which is what I have been doing all day.
Tell me, what else should I have done?
Doesn't everything die at last, and too soon?
Tell me, what is it you plan to do
with your one wild and precious life?

Mary Oliver

Your Turn

What is a miracle or mystery that you have observed? A child playing, a grandmother caring, a boy catching a ball, an animal sleeping . . .

—

Something you know and you love. Build it up using all the senses and careful concrete details. It's the detail of the observation that makes Mary Oliver's a great poem.

—

(The use of gerunds to extend the moment and active verbs to move time on is fabulous, and you should definitely try some of that.)

—

Put your own observation at the heart of your poem, and use questions, as Mary Oliver does, to frame it.

—

Who made? is a powerful question, because it invokes God. You can use that one, or something more secular:

What is this child?

Where does it come from, this love?

How does it unfold, this grace?

Make sure, though, that you are also setting your scene using concrete details.

This child, I mean, who . . .

This grandmother, who . . .

—

Now, think of some things you don't know

– the size of the universe, the right way to raise a child.

List them.

But I do know . . .

List the things you are sure of

—

And you can finish with a question to the reader.

Tell me . . . what else is there?

What else should we do?

In General: Titles

The title of a poem can be many things:

An advertisement to entice us to read the poem.
A signpost, to direct us into the matter of the poem.
A map, to locate us in time and space before we start reading the poem.
A puzzle whose solution is to be found by reading the poem.
A comment on the poem which enriches it after we've read it.

Ideally, it is all of those things.

So titles are worth spending time on – and do remember they can
be long and informative as well as short and snappy.

Home Movies

Dig deeper into your personal stock of images: both those you have filmed with your own eyes, and those we inherit from the cinema and television.

This is a wonderful poem to borrow from because it affirms personal experience.

It Ain't What You Do, It's What It Does to You

I have not bummed across America
with only a dollar to spare, one pair
of busted Levi's and a bowie knife.
I have lived with thieves in Manchester.

I have not padded through the Taj Mahal,
barefoot, listening to the space between
each footfall, picking up and putting down
its print against the marble floor. But I

skimmed flat stones across Black Moss on a day
so still I could hear each set of ripples
as they crossed. I felt each stone's inertia
spend itself against the water; then sink.

I have not toyed with a parachute cord
while perched on the lip of a light aircraft;
but I held the wobbly head of a boy
at the day centre, and stroked his fat hands.

And I guess that the lightness in the throat
and the tiny cascading sensation
somewhere inside us are both part of that
sense of something else. That feeling, I mean.

Simon Armitage

Your Turn

I have not . . .

Make a list of places you haven't been yet: the gap-year experiences you haven't had, the jumps from parachutes and white-water rides you haven't taken.

—

Remember your five senses.

There are the sights you haven't seen –

But what about tastes: the five-star meals and/or live oysters you haven't eaten, the Manhattan cocktails you are yet to sip?

Or smells? Sulphurous volcanoes, exquisite orchids, fine perfumes . . .

The feelings – cold waterfalls, hot deserts, silk sheets.

And the sounds – the orchestras, sopranos, purring engines you are yet to hear.

But I . . .

Now what about the sights, tastes, smells, sounds and feelings that you have experienced and deeply value?

—

Make your ideas into extended images – little movies – and remember to make them move. Use active verbs.

—

Now assemble your images as a series of contrasts: matching them by sense, perhaps.

—

To end your poem, you need to pick the image that means the most to you – like the wobbly head of the boy in the Armitage poem.

And maybe you can add a general statement: you can borrow 'that feeling, I mean'. If you like.

—

Azfa was sixteen when she wrote this version. Her images are so different from Armitage's that even though she leans on his structure, her poem becomes her own.

So will yours.

Fountains

I have not heard
The opera in New York

But I have heard
The bagpipes
In Scotland
An alien bird with tartan feathers
Wild as a peacock
With a mushy haggis heart.

I have not heard
The soaring Gospel

But I have heard
The Holy Quran
Its sweet zam zam water
Dripping slowly slowly
through the stream beds
of my eardrums, slipping through
my veins to my heart,
a ruby, drumming throne.

I have not heard
The President's speech,
But I have heard
My Dad's honourable advice.
His voice a messenger riding

from his mind which is
an over-flowing fountain
of knowledge, springing
from his journeys
and splashing me with wonder
from head to toe.

Azfa Awad (sixteen)

In General: How Far Can You Go?

I have one genuinely popular poem – it is read at weddings, is posted on hundreds of blogs, is multiply translated, has its own movies on YouTube and even appears on a One Direction fan site, being spoken by Louis to Harry. It's called 'Patagonia' and I nearly didn't put it into my first collection because I thought its metaphors were too personal and peculiar and no one would ever understand it. One of its images, for example, is of a barnacle pulling itself off a rock and paddling off in the coracle of itself. That is honestly a pretty odd picture but nobody, even a One Direction fan, has apparently ever had any difficulty with it.

I offer this story to anyone wondering how personal their own references can be in their images – how far they can go. Usually, as with a really good joke, the answer is 'as far as you can, as far as you dare'. Paradoxically, the most personal associations often turn out to be the most widely shared and recognizable. Presumably Hera Lindsay Bird also wondered if it was too far out to compare love to Windows 95, or Simon Armitage paused a moment over the boy with the wobbly head, but they were both right to press ahead and use them in their poem.

Take the risk. Use that far-out image, the one that seems authentic but strange to you, the one that makes you blush. It probably isn't incomprehensible, and if it really is, someone will tell you at a later stage. But resist the temptation to insert some extra lines explaining your image, because that isn't just dull, it's condescending. Remember the adage 'Never apologize, never explain': be grand and superb and confident. And if you want to write a poem beginning 'I said . . .' and ending 'I meant . . .' – please, be my guest.

Patagonia

I said *perhaps Patagonia*, and pictured
a peninsula, wide enough
for a couple of ladderback chairs
to wobble on at high tide. I thought

of us in breathless cold, facing
a horizon round as a coin, looped
in a cat's cradle strung by gulls
from sea to sun. I planned to wait

till the waves had bored themselves
to sleep, till the last clinging barnacles,
growing worried in the hush, had
paddled off in tiny coracles, till

those restless birds, your actor's hands,
had dropped slack into your lap,
until you'd turned, at last, to me.
When I spoke of Patagonia, I meant

skies all empty aching blue. I meant
years. I meant all of them with you.

Kate Clanchy

Put Your Images through the Rinse Cycle:
'A Guide to Love in Icelandic'

Rebecca Perry took a poem about love and translated it into Icelandic using Google Translate, then copied and pasted the translation, and translated that back into English. This poem keeps several of the phrases that resulted from that process.

Translation takes a literal approach to figurative language – it deconstructs your metaphors for you, and makes you think about them freshly. Romantic metaphors about shedding antler velvet and Christingle have been made blunt and strange here – but they are somehow very memorable.

Try it for yourself with one of your recent poems. This game works

A Guide to Love in Icelandic

When lemon drops stick together in a paper bag
it's like love.
There are certain risks in cooperative living,
warmth, gravitational laws, the sticky sun.
And when the lightbulb pops and explodes
it's like love.
When we are naked and heart pounding in the shower,
in the new dark afraid of being so close to water.
And it's like love
when the sun disappears from months
and when you stick cloves into an orange.
And when in the woods antlers fall from deer onto grass
it's like love.
To persist into spring when you have lost
some part of the whole self.
When you feel a chill and cover your feet
it's like love.
Suddenly you're in a movie, the breeze from an open
window isn't real, the walls are paper, food is plastic.
And it's like love
when a train stops dead in a tunnel
and when a beloved cat shows its claws.
And when tar is compressed into uniform blocks,
it's like love.
The air is all white smoke and impossible to breathe
the blocks stack to the sky.

especially well with languages with a different root to English, such as Basque or Finnish.

Once you have a translated version, pick some of the best words and phrases for your final version.

When you fall down the stairs
it's like love.
And when you are soaked through to the bones,
your clothes are a deadweight and the radiators click to life.

Rebecca Perry

Move Right into Your Metaphor:
Your Heart and My Heart

What house is your heart? This (very free) translation of the mystic Persian poet Hafiz is a great starting point for that most awful of commissions, the Valentine verse.

Your Mother and My Mother

Fear is the cheapest room in the house.
I would like to see you living
In better conditions,

For your mother and my mother
Were friends.

I know the Innkeeper
In this part of the universe.
Get some rest tonight,
Come to my verse again tomorrow.
We'll go speak to the Friend together.

I should not make any promises right now,
But I know if you
Pray
Somewhere in this world –
Something good will happen.

God wants to see
More love and playfulness in your eyes
For that is your greatest witness to Him.

Your soul and my soul
Once sat together in the Beloved's womb
Playing footsie.

Your heart and my heart
Are very, very old friends.

Khwāja Shams-ud-Dīn Muḥammad Ḥāfeẓ-e Shīrāzī (Hafiz)

Your Turn

You're writing a letter to someone you love. Borrow Hafiz's frame: which emotional room are they currently in?

And which one do you think that they belong in? Be concrete and specific. Furnish it.

What's outside the window? What is the view?

How are you going to arrange the move? Do you know the innkeeper? Will you be plumping the pillow? What would you advise they do tomorrow? And tonight?

And what about your heart and their heart? What are they?

Create a metaphor.

—

There, a poem.

Sana was only twelve, and
very dyslexic.

Brother

Friendship is the most expensive
Room in my house.
And that is where you belong.
Full of fresh flowers daily,
Diamonds for windows and a golden frame.

It has a balcony to see as far
As the park we used to play in,
The shady trees where we had ice-cream.
The courts where you beat me at tennis.
Just sit there with me.

Sana Ul-Hasan (twelve)

PERMISSION TO WRITE
Read Like a Poet

If you want to join in the conversation of poetry, you have to read and listen to lots of it. Much of your reading should be contemporary poetry. This does not mean you should not also read the classics – of course you should – but if you choose to read only, for example, nineteenth-century poetry, then your poems will be in conversation with the nineteenth century and sound as if they are. Which is fine – but don't expect to be heard so easily in the twenty-first. Contemporary poets are the voices that your voice will join; the voices of now.

Whatever you are reading, let it be like a writer, not a critic. Don't think about what is 'important' or make up hierarchies of 'best'. Let yourself love what you love: adore certain lines and poems just because they remind you of your own experiences; learn phrases by heart because they appeal to you; copy out poems that you like into a commonplace book. Be a fan: allow yourself to have a poetic crush, to put poems into other people's hands or ping them into their phone accompanied by embarrassing gifs.

Hate freely too – if a poem says nothing to you about your life, put it aside, however strongly recommended it is. If a poet's rhetorical tics or pompous diction or stereotyped characters irritate you – be enraged. Try to write down why.

Be a magpie: copy titles, ideas, line endings, rhythms, shamelessly and frequently. Notice when other writers are doing this too.

Notice: this is a conversation. Give yourself permission to join in. Reading like a writer is an important part of this exchange.

Room for Your Poems: Get Hold of Poetry

Reading your contemporaries is much easier than ever before because of the internet. You can look up any name in this book on Google and be led to videos, audio, sites such as the Poetry Foundation, the Poetry Archive and Button Poetry, and more and more poems.

It's an amazing resource, but don't let it be your only poetry experience. Both poetry anthologies and poetry collections need to be thumbed through physically to be really understood. You can't learn to place words on the page – to break a line or a stanza – unless you have held many pages in your hands and taken in how the typeface sits on them. Poems are multi-dimensional, and touch – paper – is one of their dimensions. Go to the Poetry Library in London, Edinburgh or Manchester, or the poetry section of your local library. Order stuff in. Become a buyer of poetry – there aren't enough of us. Subscribe to a magazine: *Poetry London*, *Poetry Review*, *The Rialto*. Buy a compendious anthology such as Neil Astley's *Being Alive* and let the poems in there lead you to other poems.

You'll need a poetry library of your own too – or at least a shelf to sit next to your poetry notebooks and files.

Start a commonplace book – writing out or printing poems you especially like and putting them together in a notebook. Or make an e-version on your computer.

Send poems you like to people you think will appreciate them, or stick them into cards.

Open several books at once. Look at the ways poems work together and talk to each other. Enjoy the conversation.

3
BUILDING YOUR WRITING PROCESS

Lists, Plots and Turns

Finding Your Writing Process

People talk a lot about poets 'finding a voice'. If that sounds like an intimidating concept you might prefer to focus on building up a writing process: a series of steps by which you make your writing better.

Inspiration is actually not so rare: everyone gets moments of it. The writer is the person with the confidence and patience and process to build on those moments.

Everyone also has times when they feel lost and hopeless about their work, and want to throw it away: a process can be a map in your pocket, a ladder out of the ditch.

The way writers sound in their finished work has as much to do with their process – with the way they habitually work on an impulse and push themselves through redrafts – as it does with those moments of inspiration (which is why you should also revise your *process*, from time to time, before you start sounding too much like yourself).

Learning a writing process is like learning any other process, such as how to dance: it is painful and best done by slow, exaggerated movements; in time it becomes internalized, effortless and graceful.

The slow, exaggerated movements in this chapter help you learn to structure a poem – how you put a list of images together and make it tell an emotional story.

(Growing) Your Inner Checklist:
The Furniture Game

The Furniture Game was named and invented by the great poet/ teacher Sandy Brownjohn. It's a game of question and answer: you define a feeling or idea or person by asking a series of questions which have to be answered with metaphors, all of them concrete and specific. It's named after a particularly useful question: if she/ he/they/it were a piece of furniture, what would that be?

If you are playing the Furniture Game in a group or class you can use a guessing element: one player thinks of a person known to the group. Everyone else then asks questions about the person which must be answered in metaphors. 'If this person were a dog, they would be an old, smelly Great Dane.' 'If they were an item of furniture, they'd be a battered sofa.' The first player to guess the original thing or person takes a turn to think something up. It's a compelling game, because it plays with all the images we share, and the childlike, imagistic way so many of us still see the world while pretending very hard that we don't.

You can play the Furniture Game on your own, though. Then it's more a matter of having questions in your head ready for when you experience a poetic impulse and want to build on it – e.g. when you have a strong feeling for someone and want to define it.

The central questions are:

What are they like?
What's it like?
What are you like?

Good Furniture Game questions include:

If it were an animal?
A breed of dog?
An insect?
A bird?
A tree?
A flower?
A season?
A phase of the moon?
A body of water?
A sky?
A cloud?
A boat?
A form of public transport?
A car?
An horizon?
A large machine?
A sort of clock?
A kitchen implement?
A drink?
An art movement?
A vista?
A time of day?

Or you could take inspiration from Simon Armitage's famous poetic portrait.

Not the Furniture Game

His hair was a crow fished out of a blocked chimney
and his eyes were boiled eggs with the tops hammered in
and his blink was a cat flap
and his teeth were bluestones or the Easter Island statues
and his bite was a perfect horseshoe.
His nostrils were both barrels of a shotgun, loaded.
And his mouth was an oil exploration project gone bankrupt
and his smile was a caesarean section
and his tongue was an iguanodon
and his whistle was a laser beam
and his laugh was a bad case of kennel cough.
He coughed, and it was malt whisky.
And his headaches were Arson in Her Majesty's Dockyards
and his arguments were outboard motors strangled with
    fishing line
and his neck was a bandstand
and his Adam's apple was a ball cock
and his arms were milk running off from a broken bottle.
His elbows were boomerangs or pinking shears.
And his wrists were ankles
and his handshakes were puff adders in the bran tub
and his fingers were astronauts found dead in their spacesuits
and the palms of his hands were action paintings
and both thumbs were blue touchpaper.
And his shadow was an opencast mine.
And his dog was a sentry box with no-one in it
and his heart was a first world war grenade discovered by children

and his nipples were timers for incendiary devices
and his shoulder blades were two butchers at the meat cleaving
    competition
and his belly button was the Falkland Islands
and his private parts were the Bermuda triangle
and his backside was a priest hole
and his stretchmarks were the tide going out.
The whole system of his blood was Dutch elm disease.
And his legs were depth charges
and his knees were fossils waiting to be tapped open
and his ligaments were rifles wrapped in oilcloth under the
    floorboards
and his calves were the undercarriages of Shackletons.
The balls of his feet were where meteorites had landed
and his toes were a nest of mice under the lawn mower.
And his footprints were Vietnam
and his promises were hot air balloons floating off over the trees
and his one-liners were footballs through other people's windows
and his grin was the Great Wall of China as seen from the moon
and the last time they talked, it was apartheid.

She was a chair, tipped over backwards
with his donkey jacket on her shoulders.

They told him,
and his face was a hole
where the ice had not been thick enough to hold her.

Simon Armitage

Your Turn

Try a Furniture Game Portrait.

Write yourself a list of Furniture Game questions down one side of
a piece of paper:

If they were a dog
A sofa
A kind of weather

Add some from the Armitage poem:

and his grin is
and his footprints are
and his promises

Now, think of someone you have strong feelings about, whatever
those feelings are – love, hate, longing, lust . . .

Write their name on the top of your piece of paper.

Then, working quickly, answer the Furniture Game questions
about them.

You can't stop to think, you have to just keep writing, line to line.

You have to fill the whole page.

Leave the list for a bit while you do something else, then come
back and have a read.

The images that embarrass you or surprise you are probably
keepers.

The ones which seem familiar, or borrowed, or repetitive probably aren't.

Now you can start to rewrite.

Are you going to write it *to* someone – *You are*?

Or *about* someone – *he/she/they is/are*?

Or even use a name or title – *My Boss, Mrs Jones*.

As you rewrite, think about concrete details, and the senses, and making it yours – but also start to think about the order of the images.

Armitage's portrait sweeps from the head to the feet of his subject, creating a strong visual image, but it also moves inward, becoming more frightening and sadder.

What mood do you want to create in your poem?

What feeling do you want to leave your reader with?

You may well find that you have created a darker or sadder or funnier or lonelier portrait than you intended. Resist the temptation to tidy up the feelings. (Tidying up the gerunds and pruning the intensifiers is always fine.) The poem is telling you something, and it is probably right.

In General: First Lines: No Time to Clear Your Throat

It's very easy, as you draft, to stick to the line order in which you first wrote your poem – it can just feel so certain and inspired – especially that first line.

Which is why it is always worth giving your first line a little extra attention as you draft.

Try reading the poem without it.

Does it still make sense?

If so – Is your first line a throat-clearing?

Is it trying to claim your audience's attention in some way – as if you didn't deserve it?

Is it trying to explain something that you feel the audience won't understand?

Think about the poem as a speaker: people who explain things too much or who make a special claim on your attention aren't usually the sort you're interested in.

No one is interested in a throat-clearing. You should do that before you go on stage.

Make your poem into a confident, attractive, prepared, possibly mysterious speaker. Cut the opening back to the point where the action starts.

If there is still a vital piece of information to be given – *this is the last time I saw my lover, this is a winter poem, this is a poem about a Japanese word* – try putting it in the title.

(Silhouette) Self-Portrait in a List:
'I Want the Confidence of'

This poem, by a Jamaican British d/Deaf poet, may seem on first reading to be an effortless, even random list of visual images but, in fact, it is cunningly structured and gives us a detailed portrait of the speaker, standing in the shadows, defined in silhouette.

The poet wants, he says (and the word 'wants' can also mean 'lacks'), 'confidence' – a quality he associates, through a series of gleaming images, with empowered white people, the ones who talk in the quiet coach, who know they will be seen and heard, are named after saints. The poet himself is revealed in glimpses: stirring his coffee as he is probed, watching people cross the road to avoid him.

I Want the Confidence of

Salvador Dalí in a 1950s McDonald's advert,
of red gold and green ties
on shantytown Dapper dandies, of Cuba Gooding Jr
in a strip club shouting SHOW ME THE MONEY,
of the woman on her phone in the quiet coach,
of knowing you'll be seen and served,
that no one will cross the road when they see you,
the sun shining through the gaps in the buildings,
a glass ceiling in a restaurant
where knives and spoons wink,
a polite pint and a cheeky cigarette, tattoos
on the arms, trains that blur the whole city without delay.
I want the confidence of the coffee bean in the body,
a surface that doesn't need scratching;
I want to be fluent in confidence so large it speaks from its own sky.
At the airport I want my confidence to board
without investigations, to sit in foreign cafes
without a silver spoon in a teacup clinking
into sunken places, of someone named after a saint,
of Matthew the deaf footballer who couldn't hear
to pass the ball, but still ran the pitch, of leather jackets in the teeth
of hot combs, rollin' roadmen and rubber.
I don't want my confidence to lie:
it has to mean helium balloons in any shape or colour,
it has to mean rubber tree in rain; make it
my sister leaving home for university, my finally sober father,
my mother becoming a circus clown.

As the poem goes on, the poet starts producing positive images instead of negatives. The deaf footballer, the rubber tree in the rain, and then the family images – 'my finally sober father' – all contribute to an imagistic colouring-in of the poet, and the poem ends with a boy busking to his own dark reflection, finding his confidence in his own poem. Which is of course what you are going to do next.

There is such a thing as a key confidently cut
that accepts the locks it doesn't fit.
Call it a boy busking on the canal path singing
to no one but the bridges
and the black water under them.

Raymond Antrobus

Your Turn

What do you want – or lack?

Confidence?

Faith?

Friendship?

Intimacy? Lightness?

The list could easily get alarming.

Actually, alarming can be good.

Try to choose your most scary option.

That's your title.

I want the faith/warmth/agency of . . .

—

Now, get out your Furniture Game list –

If it were an animal

insect

drink

landscape

machine . . .

—

Try to work quickly, associating freely. Let yourself build a long, long list.

—

Now leave it for a bit –

In General: Leaving a Poem to Rise

Poems are like bread. They need to be kneaded into dough, left to rise, then kneaded down again before being shaped and baked.

Don't be afraid to walk away from the draft of a poem for several hours, days or weeks. You will see it more clearly when you return, and work on it more effectively.

In baking, this is called proving. The better the grain of the bread, and the higher quality the flour, the more kneading and rising are required.

The more times you prove and knead your poem, the more you will notice, and not only will your poem get stronger, so will your writing process.

If you rush a poem out of the house – declare it finished, perform it, share it with a friend – you may well see something later that isn't quite right, and regret it.

As bakers will tell you, if you bake too soon, you get a thick crust and a mushy middle, and sometimes the whole thing collapses.

Your Turn

After a break, look at your list.

—

What order are you going to choose for your images? That's what will make the meaning of the poem.

—

Linnet wrote this poem after reading Raymond Antrobus's poem, and she echoed his order by opening with the bright images, moving on to more sombre ones, and ending with the human herself.

—

As an order, it works very well. Why not try it?

—

Some metaphors might not work here. Weed them out, or save them for another poem.

I want the faith

of the glass cup that merely bounced
when I dropped it on the parquet floor,
of the clear liquid that barely spilled,

of the weeds that survived the summer,
of the tiny light bulbs from the Physics Practical
that still flicker months later,

of the streetlamps that turn on by themselves
at dusk; of the lady who paints the beach
in the rain, her acrylic turning to watercolour

of those tins of emulsion that don't bother
with a sample, that describe their colour
with words. Mine fail me.

Linnet Drury (fifteen)

In General: Last Lines: Keep Out of the Pulpit

Last lines are so important – the place where the whole poem is headed, where twists are delivered, the ones which echo in the mind.

Very often, too, they are the ones we have in mind from the first, are most proud of, and which have the loudest iambic rhythm.

Before you sign off on a line like this, though, just try reading your poem aloud without it.

Is anything lost?

Does your last line, or last few lines, explain your poem rather than move the action forward?

Many beginning poets feel the need to explain their point explicitly, as if their poem and images were not clear enough on their own. And also because a last line can offer a generalizing, preacher moment, it is always so tempting to pop into the pulpit.

Try your poem without that grand last line. It may well, paradoxically, sound more confident.

Rhythmic Lists:
'Wasp'

Because they are repetitive, lists are also inherently rhythmic. This short poem uses that quality to echo the sound of the wasp and to make us scared and irritated. Even though the poem is short, it still alters cleverly in tone, from the gentle 'nibbler' to the much more emotive 'mounter' and painful 'pocket knife'. The ordering also implies a story, from buzzing to sting.

Wasp

little lion. little nibbler.
little face dunker. little duck.
little clinging cashew nut.
little rummager, sifting for gold.
little hovercraft. little clamberer.
little engine. little warrior, little armoured.
little snail-slime wings.
little nuzzler, nuzzling a neck.
little alien, little feeler, little zebra.
little dinosaur legs.
little sycophant. little mounter.
little vampire, little pollen sucking bead.
little pocket knife.

Rebecca Perry

Your Turn

Try a short, repetitive, rhythmic list for yourself.

Think of something or somebody you want to describe, something that's on your mind, that you have strong, not necessarily happy, feelings about.

Play a round of the Furniture Game with it: if it were a boat, yacht, animal, sunset, colour . . .

Now think of a two-beat adjective – busy, darkest, smallest, nearest, crying, noisy – that you can repeat.

Put the two together and make a list.

Remember all your best list rules. Where does it start, where does it end?

Sound out your own rhythm. And away you go.

A Turn for the Better:
Build in a Volta

Here is more inspiration for a long, listing, Furniture Game poem. This one has the 'I want' verb too. The cow is a fantastic symbol for feelings of shame, and each stanza builds it up with more detail.

Cow

I want to be a cow
and not my mother's daughter.
I want to be a cow
and not in love with you.
I want to feel free to feel calm.
I want to be a cow who never knows
the kind of love you 'fall in love with' with;
a queenly cow, with hips as big and sound
as a department store,
a cow the farmer milks on bended knee,
who when she dies will feel dawn
bending over her like lawn to wet her lips.

I want to be a cow,
nothing fancy –
a cargo of grass,
a hammock of soupy milk
whose floating and rocking and dribbling's undisturbed
by the echo of hooves to the city;
of crunching boots;
of suspicious-looking trailers parked on verges;
of unscrupulous restaurant-owners
who stumble, pink-eyed, from stale beds
into a world of lobsters and warm telephones;
of streamlined Japanese freighters
ironing the night,
heavy with sweet desire like bowls of jam.

The poem does more than list, though – it has a turn, a volta.

In the last stanza, it stops soliloquizing – addressing the reader, or the air – and turns to speak to a 'you' who has black stockings and a hat, who wants the poet to come home. A mother. The change of tone and use of the imperative suddenly make the poem more dramatic and funny.

Lots of poems have voltas, because it's highly effective, like a change of tempo in music or switch of direction in a dance.

The Tibetans have 85 words for states of consciousness.
This dozy cow I want to be has none.
She doesn't speak.
She doesn't do housework or worry about her appearance.
She doesn't roam.
Safe in her fleet
of shorn-white-bowl-like friends,
she needs, and loves, and is loved by,
only this –
the farm I want to be a cow on too.

Don't come looking for me.
Don't come walking out into the bright sunlight
looking for me,
black in your gloves and stockings and sleeves
and large hat.
Don't call the tractorman.
Don't call the neighbours.
Don't make a special fruit-cake for when I come home:
I'm not coming home.
I'm going to be a cowman's counted cow.
I'm going to be a cow
and you won't know me.

Selima Hill

Your Turn

Try a version of 'Cow' and make a volta work for you.

Start with 'I want to be' and your Furniture Game list – animal, plant, drink, flower, machine . . .

Try a list of nots

Try a list of don'ts

Try 'I'm going'

Now, leave your poem to rise . . .

—

When you come back, see if you can see a plot twist, a change in your poem.

—

Arrange your lines so the twist is stronger and clearer.

—

There. A volta!

—

Iesha wanted to be the moon.

Moon

I want to be the moon
and not in Year 11. I want
to be admired for who I am
and not for the box you fit me in.
I want to be the moon so I can
fade away when you're speaking.
I want to be endless and infinite.
Everywhere – not stationary for hours
on end. I would like to be invisible,
forgotten with the seasons.

You with your a squared plus
b squared equals c squared,
your aller, être, your infinitives
and ongoing dictatorships.
Don't try to speak to me, because
I'm slipping out of here.
Don't gaze at me in awe
when you looked through me before.
I am going to be the moon,
and you won't recognise me.

Iesha Jennings (fifteen)

Oh! Lists of Three and Their Enduring Magic!

Amplifying, attention-grabbing, rhythmic lists of three are politicians' and advertisers' rhetorical figure of choice. Which can take the shine off them . . . but, as Frank O'Hara points out, not much, because poetry magic is strong.

Again, this poem is very short, but it still uses a change of tone. In fact, there is a full volta after the stanza break: instead of talking about sweets and harmonicas we are suddenly talking about poetry, war, death and eternity.

Today

Oh! kangaroos, sequins, chocolate sodas!
You really are beautiful! Pearls,
harmonicas, jujubes, aspirins! all
the stuff they've always talked about

still makes a poem a surprise!
These things are with us every day
even on beachheads and biers. They
do have meaning. They're strong as rocks.

Frank O'Hara

Your Turn

Frank O'Hara's poem is sublimely easy to copy

—

Just read it through a few times.

—

Then shake out your own list of three favourite words, then another three.

—

You're going to write these words a hymn of praise: an ode.

—

So you'll have to start yourself off in ode-mode with the word 'O', even if you remove it later.

—

The rhythm will follow, as it did for Freya.

Ode

Sherbet lemons, marigolds, sweet tea – why
Are there never enough velvet words for them?
It is thought that to speak of peanut butter
And the clatter of spoons in a drawer of receipts
Is unfathomable. Not to me. I could natter
Of their glory all evening. I could talk about
Bubble baths, and magpies, and your heart

Of course, hung up there on a coat hanger.

Freya Carter (fourteen)

In General: Seeing Your Poem Freshly

Keep on working on the endless problem of seeing your own work freshly.

We all tend to read what we *meant* to write, not what we actually put on the paper.

To make your poem fresh in your mind and eye, try:

Reading it aloud (always best).

Or taking all the line breaks out and reading it as prose.

Or running the word count and then reducing it by a random number, say seven.

Printing it out.

Changing the font.

And reading it aloud again.

The Heart: A List

Take all the skills you've learned and make a version of one of these poems about the heart.

Play the Furniture Game, like Simon Armitage, and make a list of metaphors.

Edit it into your best list, like Raymond Antrobus.

Use a volta, like Selima Hill.

Harness rhythm, like Rebecca Perry.

And go.

My Heart

Every image here is fully imagined. Everything smells, tastes and sticks to you with plastic gloves. And the ending is a spiral of voltas.

That Mississippi chicken shack.
That initial-scarred tabletop,
that tiny little dance floor to the left of the band.
That kiosk at the mall selling caramels and kitsch.
That tollbooth with its white-plastic-gloved worker
handing you your change.
That phone booth with the receiver ripped out.
That dressing room in the fetish boutique,
those curtains and mirrors.
That funhouse, that horror, that soundtrack of screams.
That putti-filled heaven raining gilt from the ceiling.
That haven for truckers, that bottomless cup.
That biome. That wilderness preserve.
That landing strip with no runway lights
where you are aiming your plane,
imagining a voice in the tower.
imagining a tower.

Kim Addonizio

There is something fragile about each of Christina Rossetti's images. The shoot needs watering, the bough is bending, and shells are usually dead. It's part of what makes this poem so tender and memorable.

A Birthday

My heart is like a singing bird
    Whose nest is in a water'd shoot;
My heart is like an apple-tree
    Whose boughs are bent with thickset fruit;
My heart is like a rainbow shell
    That paddles in a halcyon sea;
My heart is gladder than all these
    Because my love is come to me.

Raise me a dais of silk and down;
    Hang it with vair and purple dyes;
Carve it in doves and pomegranates,
    And peacocks with a hundred eyes;
Work it in gold and silver grapes,
    In leaves and silver fleurs-de-lys;
Because the birthday of my life
    Is come, my love is come to me.

Christina Rossetti

Helen was a student at my school. She came up with this list in less than half an hour. Adults probably have to try harder.

Ellipse

My heart is a folly left
  to its own foolishness, becoming overgrown.
My heart is a circus cage without a lion
  a sawdust ring with empty footsteps.
My heart is a quince tree, gold
  and bitter fruit.
My heart is a bottle cast back in the sea
  cork unstopped and message read.
My heart is a stopped clock
  that lets the hours roll out unattended.
My heart is a horseshoe shape
  with its own conflicting myth of which way up.
My heart is a sonnet which unravels itself
  in spools of listening, hearing.
My heart is a bird that has lost its voice.
  An empty bubble of speech
  An ellipse. Eclipsed
  by words unheard.
All living things and objects talk, I think;
  but some have louder voices.

Helen Woods (fourteen)

In General: Are You Stuck but Know that There is More Poem to Write?

Maybe you've started at the end of your poem.

Poems often have a starting point in your mind.

A phrase that seems to be a line, that sounds like a poem – something resonant, probably rhythmic, often iambic . . .

'*That biome. That wilderness preserve*', for instance, in Kim Addonizio's poem.

Because that is where your poem begins for you, it's only natural to put that line at the start of your poem.

But if Addonizio had begun her poem '*That biome. That wilderness preserve*', she wouldn't have been able to carry on. Where can we go from the wilderness preserve? Only somewhere tamer.

That resonant, inspired phrase may well be a last line, not a first one.

Try moving the line further down the page.

Now see what sort of a poem you have to write to get there.

It might even be a title – try it.

Believe in Your Future and Your Past

Learning to write regularly, which in practice means rewriting regularly, can be even harder than writing for the first time. Now you have to believe in longer-term processes. You have to save work for later. You have to dig up lines you've already written and improve them. You have to build a bridge across an impossible gap in a poem.

It's hard. So hard that it's sometimes easier to lose work, or not find the time to look at it. You might accuse yourself of laziness – but ask yourself if it's really that, or fear. Fear that the poem is no good 'really'. Fear that if it is good, this is an accident, and you will spoil or lose the poem if you touch it. Fear that you are not worth the effort.

All writers face this sort of fear. Here are reminders to help you round it.

Remember . . .

You Can't Lose Your Poem (we have the technology)

Remind yourself that your computer has a 'save as' button, or that there is room in a folder for as many versions of a poem as you like. Even if you have only written four or five poems, start a 'Drafts' folder for your older versions, physical, electronic or both. Now you can experiment – you know you can always go back to that first draft, safe in your folder.

You Don't Need to Use a Line Just Because it's Good – It Can Go in the Lost Lines Folder

Create a 'Lost Lines' folder for images and lines that look and sound good, but don't fit in the poem you wrote them for. It can be physical or electronic or both. If you keep the lines safe, they will find a home one day – perhaps years from now.

You've Got Time

You don't need to put all your best ideas and everything you have ever felt in one poem – you will be allowed to write other poems. You don't need to finish anything in a hurry, either. Most poets take a year to finish off a poem.

Strengthening Your Process is Valuable in Itself

Even if you seem to be going round in circles, and have fewer poems today than you had last week, you are still learning. It's a bit like playing tennis. You have to keep practising your swing, or the day when the perfect ball arrives you won't be ready to smash it.

Above All – Believe in Your Own Future

You will still be writing in a year. You will be able to sort that poem out. You, and your poem, are worth the time and effort.

Your Poetry Place, Your Poetry Palace

Now you have a poetry library, a folder for finished work, a folder of drafts, and a 'Lost Lines' folder. Even if it's very small, or virtual, it's a nice place to go.

Your folder of 'best' poems is valued, shining and perfect.
Your 'Drafts' folder is a messy, creative haven.
Your 'Lost Lines' folder is crazy.
Your commonplace book is bulging with thoughts.

As you grow confident in your writing process, try visiting every day, even if just for a few minutes, to talk to your poems.

4 SUMMONING SPELLS

Elegies, Letters, Odes
and Things that Get in the Way

Now you have written so much, and gained so much control over your writing, you can start to do magic.

One of poetry's most ancient purposes is to summon up and commemorate the lost. This chapter offers you some classic forms – elegies, odes, letters – in contemporary form, and gives you the chance to write your own.

As you start dealing with more complex, personal material, you may well find yourself stuck in your poem and your drafting process in new ways. Interspersed in the chapter are some of the most common reasons for these feelings, and some solutions.

I Don't Remember (except the images)

This short poem by
Tagore, the national poet
of Bangladesh,
commemorates his
mother, who he lost
before he was three. It's
exquisite and original and
profound and memorable.
It's also simple: just a list
of three sensual images.

Remember

I don't remember my mother
just sometimes when I'm playing
a tune seems to hum in my ear,
the tune of a song that she used to sing
while pushing the swing of my cradle.

I don't remember my mother
but when in the early autumn morning
the smell of the shiuli flowers floats
from the morning service in temple
that dew-wet air smells to me like my mother.

I don't remember my mother
but when from my bedroom window I send
my eyes up the blue of the distant sky,
I feel that my mother's gaze on my face
has spread all over the sky.

Rabindranath Tagore

Rukiya's poem, written while reading a lot of Tagore, is for her mother country of Bangladesh. This 'I don't remember' is also the polite denial of the migrant, reassuring their new country that yes, they belong here, now. Her poem, like Tagore's, draws on very early, sensual memories – the mango juice, the 'comforting garment' of the warmth, the 'tipa tapa' of the rain – and on a huge loss.

My Mother Country

I don't remember her
In the summer,
Lagoon water sizzling,
The kingfisher leaping,
Or even the sweet honey mangoes
They tell me I used to love.
I don't remember
Her comforting garment,
Or her saps of date trees,
Providing the meagre earnings
For those farmers
Out there
In the gulf
Under the calidity of the sun,
Or the mosquitoes
Droning in the monsoon,
Or the tipa tapa of the rain,
On the tin roofs,
Dripping on the window,
I think.

Rukiya Khatun (seventeen)

Your Turn

I don't remember is a magical way to frame a poem.

It gives it irony and dramatic tension at once, while also plunging us into the deep past.

This works best for an early memory: a person or place, or person-and-place you lost in childhood.

—

Grandparents perhaps – or just a holiday house you stopped visiting.

—

Think about the sounds, smells and tastes of that place.

—

Make sure all your memories are concrete – no abstract nouns wanted in here.

—

Now try a poem:

—

I don't remember my grandmother

Just the scent . . .

—

I don't remember that house

Just the taste of . . .

—

I don't remember that country

Not even the sound of . . .

—

Run through your five senses:

What are the smells,

sounds,

touches,

tastes

and sights you associate with that loss?

What colour?

What flower?

What sky?

—

As you edit, remember everything you have learned about storytelling: contrast, light and shade, rhythm, the holding of a mystery, the placing of an ending.

—

You could choose to end with a big image – all over the sky – like Tagore.

Or a return to the present like Rukiya's 'I think'.

As you edit, listen to the sounds you have created. Both these poems create very strong sound-echoes.

In General: How True is Your Truth?

As you are writing a poem drawing on memories, you may well find yourself including scenes or using details that didn't actually happen to you personally, or which didn't occur at the exact moment you are talking about – for example, you may find yourself writing a poem in which you sail out to a picnic that happened when you were eight, in the boat you didn't get into till you were eleven, during a storm that comes from one of your aunt's stories about your cousin, and with a friend who was never there at all – but somehow it all coalesces authentically around a feeling and makes a truth.

As you draft and redraft you may notice more of these moments, and even that you are actually making things up. This may stop you writing, or drafting, as you worry that you are creating a lie.

Try to fight this anxiety and keep writing.

Authenticity is different from accuracy. Details seem authentic when they convey emotions and atmosphere, not because they were actually there.

When in doubt, try to be true to the poem, not the experience. Let the poem tell its truth, even (especially) when it's a difficult one.

Missing People 1:
The Elegy

This beautiful contemporary elegy evokes a lost person through a series of clear, concrete images.

Jade

You are a box of letters underneath my bed
Nearly burned through by grieving candles. You are the wax
I spilled, gone cold now, cold dust-ash. You open all the letters
That come to the house, you are the eyes that pore over
All of my poems. I would wish you away
But you are forever somehow away from me.

The things you couldn't know for sure about me
When you lived could fill a small box. They collect
Moments of deep uncertainty still, and dust, cheap
tributes. Your letters always said so much more about me
than yourself – they haunt me, little white rabbits.

Relics of the secrets that once lingered on our clothes,
When we went home to our parents –
When I feel, see, imagine,
The shape of your warm lips.

Melissa Lee-Houghton

Your Turn

Think of someone you have lost.

(NB It doesn't need to be death. It might be someone who moved house, or who ended your relationship, or who simply changed until your friendship didn't work any more.)

But it does need to be someone you loved.

When do you think of them, and why?

Get out your Furniture Game lists and run through them.

What chair is this person? What weather?

What bus or car? What kind of light?

What coat? What pair of boots?

What walk? What landmark? What building?

What scent? What smell?

What time of day?

What body part? What daily action?

Where do you put all your memories of this person?

What box or book does it all go in?

Can you close it?

—

And borrow Melissa Lee-Houghton's poem to write up your list.

Just begin:

You're . . .

Remember our rules about light and shade and telling a story.

Remember the Furniture Game.

Try putting your images in an order that suggests a sequence of actions: opening a drawer and looking for something, putting on a coat and going for a walk, for instance.

End with an image of packing away and closing.

In General: Sounds that Tell You Something

As you edit your poem (remembering all the time to be concrete, specific, to use active verbs, avoid gerunds, control your list), listen to the sounds you are using. Elegies call up 'o's of grief in us – your poem may well be full of them.

Melissa Lee-Houghton's poem is full of half-rhymed kisses: *dust, box, rabbis, secrets, relics, lips.*

You may find you have used a rhyme or two in your poem without specially intending to. If you have, look where they fall – you may well have linked two references to a person, or a thing with a mood. You might want to move the rhyming words to the end of the poem for a sense of closure – or that might be a terrible idea. The whole point, as in 'Jade', might be the lack of closure. But all the options are worth considering. Your poem is worth listening to.

Missing People 2:
Ode to a Magical Object

Sometimes, there is a single magical object which evokes a whole person. For the poet W. S. Graham, mourning his friend the expressionist painter Roger Hilton, it was a watch which conjured up their shared bohemian life in the Cornish village of Botallack.

Lines on Roger Hilton's Watch

Which I was given because
I loved him, and we had
Terrible times together.

O tarnished ticking time
Piece with your bent hand,
You must be used to being
Looked at suddenly
In the middle of the night
When he switched the light on
Beside his bed. I hope
You told him the best time
When he lifted you up
To meet the Hilton gaze.

I lift you up from the mantel
Piece here in my house
Wearing your verdigris.
At least I keep you wound
And put my ear to you
To hear Botallack tick.

You realise your master
Has relinquished you
And gone to lie under
The ground at St Just.

Tell me the time. The time
Is Botallack o'clock.
This is the dead of night.

He switches the light on
To find a cigarette
And pour himself a Teachers
He picks me up and holds me
Near his lonely face

To see my hands. He thinks
He is not being watched.

The images of his dream
Are still about his face
As he spits and tries not
To remember where he was.

I am only a watch
And pray time hastes away.
I think I am running down.

Watch, it is time I wound
You up again. I am
Very much not your dear
Last master but we had
Terrible times together.

W. S. Graham

Your Turn

Think of an object that you associate strongly with one particular person – a watch, a pack of cards, a bag, a hat, a shoe . . .

Can you actually hold it or see it? Do. If you can't, picture it strongly in your mind's eye.

Pick it up, physically or in your mind. What is that like? How big is it, how much does it weigh, what does it smell of?

You're talking to it.

Tell it about why you have picked it up or are looking at it.

How did your lost person relate to it?

Remember to keep everything concrete: smells, tastes, touches, sounds.

What does the object know?

What does it remember?

—

The object is going to talk.

How does it see your face?

Does it remember your friend?

What does it pray for?

—

Put the object down. Where?

What will happen now?

—

Edit your poem, using everything you know about storytelling and contrast, light and shade.

Be extra careful to cut out abstract words and superfluous adjectives – this sort of emotional material is enough on its own.

You will probably find that the mesmeric ticking sounds and sombre tone of the Graham poem have transferred themselves to yours.

In General: Does Your Poem Want to Be About Something (or Someone) Else?

Sometimes (often), the poem you are writing turns out not to be on the subject you set out to talk about.

It may even be straying into something you definitely didn't want to write about.

Now it's tempting to tidy the poem up. Tie it tightly to the subject you laid out for yourself. Cut off all those wayward branches.

Don't. A forced poem, like a plant, will have an unlikely colour and a weak stem. It may not even be able to stand up on its own.

So why not let the poem appearing on your page be the poem you are writing.

Follow the poem down its own path. Let it grow into its own form.

Remember, you can always change the title . . .

Missing People 3:
The Letter

The letter is another classic poetic form. Directing the piece to someone else gives dramatic tension, backstory and energy, while also seeming very natural. After all, doesn't everyone long to write to someone we miss?

Rebecca Perry puts this classic form to an unusual use – celebrating female friendship. It was originally published in an anthology called *Best Friends Forever*, edited by Amy Key.

Soup Sister

And, of course,
it bothers me greatly that I can't know
the quality of the light where you are.
How your each day pans out,
how the breeze lifts the dry leaves from the street
or how the street pulls away from the rain.

Last week I passed a tree
that was exactly you in tree form,
with a kind look and tiny sub-branches
like your delicate wrists.

Six years ago we were lying
in a dark front room on perpendicular sofas,
so hungover that our skin hurt to touch.
How did we always manage
to be heartbroken at the same time?

I could chop, de-seed and roast
a butternut squash for dinner
in the time it took you to shower.

Steam curtained the windows, whiting out
the rain, which hit the house sideways.
One of us, though I forget who, said
do you think women are treated like bowls

waiting to be filled with soup?
And the other one said, *of course.*

Now the world is too big,
and it's sinking and rising
and stretching out its back bones.

The rivers are too wild,
the mountains are so so old
and it's all laid out arrogantly between us.
My friend, how long do you stand
staring at the socks in your drawer
lined up neat as buns in a bakery,
losing track of time and your place in the world,
in the (custardy light of a) morning?

Rebecca Perry

Your Turn

Write a sister poem for 'Soup Sister'.

—

Start by thinking of someone you miss.

Picture them in your mind's eye – a good, strong image.

Where did you go together?

What did you do?

What places do you associate with them?

You could look at a photograph.

When you're sure of your ground, borrow stanza openings from 'Soup Sister' to get you writing about them.

—

Last week I passed a tree that was exactly you in tree form . . .

What triggers a thought of them? What object, plant, animal, music, scent, makes you think of them? Perry's fanciful but piercing tree comparison lets you know that it is okay to be far out.

Six years ago . . .

When you think of you two together what comes to mind?

What food, for instance? What weather? What time of day?

Write down the story.

—

One of us, though I forget who, said . . .

What were the phrases you often used together? Write them down,
even if they seem silly.

—

Now the world –

Where is your friend now? What is between you? Use a metaphor
or two.

—

And of course . . .

Is there something so strong in your friendship that you don't even
need to mention it?

Mention it now.

—

My friend, how long . . .

Close your letter with a question and an image of how you are now.

—

When you edit this poem, you may want to move the stanzas
around to tell your best story. Don't be afraid to cut. Listen to your
own sounds, and beware of extra adjectives and abstract nouns.

In General: Poems Have Plots

Poems have plots, just like stories or novels.

That is, they start at a certain point and take you somewhere else.

Sometimes, the plot is a big, obvious one, like the story of Sir Patrick Spens in the famous ballad. More often, in contemporary poems, it's a small one: someone changes their mind; the reader takes a journey into a foreign experience; the reader gets to know someone.

But even if the plot is super tiny, and made up of a list, it has to have tension. We have to wonder about something.

Why else would you keep reading?

So check your poem for plot, just as you would a story. Is there a mystery at the start? Do we finish somewhere different? Are we curious all the way through? If not, sort it out.

'My Blue Hen' doesn't
seem to be a letter poem
at first – but it reveals
itself at the end. The
poem is directed to a
'you': 'a high note, a
summer lightning storm
of a man'. The fact that it
is spoken to a distressed
animal adds another layer
of drama and tenderness.
There are numerous
magical lists in this poem
too, and sensual images,
and play of light and
shade – in fact, it adds up
to a magical formula for
writing a poem.

My Blue Hen

I sing to my blue hen. I fold her wings
against my body. The fox has had her lover,
stealing through the rough grass,
the washed sky. I tell her, I am the blue heron
the hyacinth macaw. We have
a whispered conversation in French. I tell her
the horse, the ox, the lion, are all in the stars
at different times in our lives. I tell her there are
things even the sea can't do, like come in when
it's going out. I tell her my heart is a kayak
on wild water, a coffin, and a ship in full sail.
I tell her there is no present time,
an entire field of dandelions will give her
a thousand different answers. I tell her
a dog can be a lighthouse, a zebra finch can
dream its song, vibrate its throat while sleeping.
I tell her how the Mayan midwife sings each child
into its own safe song. Tonight, the moon holds back
the dark. I snag my hair on the plum trees. I tell her
I could've been a tree, if you'd held me here long enough.
I stroke her neck. She makes a bubbling sound,
her song of eggs and feathers. I tell her you were
a high note, a summer lightning storm of a man.

Ann Gray

Your Turn

You're talking to someone or something that can't understand you or answer back. An animal, a sleeping person, a baby, even a tree or field.

I talk to . . .

Tell us who or what it is, and why you are talking.

Start with some nonsense – *I am the hyacinth macaw . . .*

Tell it some stories in another language – which one?

Tell it something about the stars.

About the sea.

About your heart.

About time.

Tell it some more nonsense – some of your favourite facts, perhaps.

Contrast that with a bit of reality – remind us where you and the creature are.

Let the creature make some sort of reply – *her song of eggs and feathers.*

Now, tell her a secret. Just one.

—

There is your poem.

This response to 'My Blue Hen' is by Sally Davis, rocket scientist and dyslexic poet. Sally did not start writing poetry till her thirties. Her poem has a dramatic speaker: someone making a chair.

Chair

First I shape the wood with song: draw out
her grain. We speak in creaks and silence,
in nattering streams. I curl back pages,
tak tak tak, and read to her of blue skies

filtered down through leaves, of peeling
silver bark. The kiss of moss. The bees.
Her breath is an ocean. I whisper to the tide,
tell her that my heart is a coracle, a clean stroke

through the water, a fishing net flung wide.
I brush out moonlight with these smith-forged
tools and pin her hair with stars. Time has many
hands to fingerprint each tree, and many arms,

and many legs, striding from me. I tell her how
the Utku-Inuit have no word for guilt. How Greek
separates space and manner in the verb *to float*,
so that the bottle must enter a cave, floating, and

this chair is carved from the forest, singing,
long true notes from the plane. The trees have
many words for love. They are leaves. Sit,
and let the seasons pull their blanket round you.

Sally Davis

In General: The Storyboard Test

As you redraft, it is always worth asking yourself:
Who is speaking this poem?
Where are they standing?
And how does the reader know?

Poems are voices – someone is speaking them, though not always the poet – and they will be more powerful if that voice is coherent and rooted. This does not mean 'single' or 'static' – poems spoken by plural voices are fantastic, and a voice can certainly rove about – just that we should be able to add up who is speaking and from where. In 'My Blue Hen', it becomes dramatically clear: it's a woman, in the orchard, at night, with hair that tangles. In dramatic monologues we get even more detail. In 'Soup Sister', we walk with the poet along the road, and stand at the drawer folding socks with her.

If your poem is like this – if it is dramatic – make sure that the drama is on the page, not just in your head. Try thinking what the storyboard (visual plan) for a video of your poem would look like. What would be in the opening and closing sequences? Do they let us know who the speaker is? Is all this information in your poem, or in your head? If it's not in the poem, sort it out – it's probably just a matter of a few visual or sensual details – some hair, a sock.

Remember that the speaker and the scenes she creates are different. A speaker can range all over the world – look at the way the poet in 'My Blue Hen' takes us to the Amazon and across oceans. But she does so from a coherent place. A ranging speaker plus a ranging set of images is simply confusing: imagine if the speaker in 'My Blue Hen' was speaking to us from her farmhouse, her childhood bedroom and her adult holiday home while also recounting her conversation with the hen. You wouldn't be able to make a film of that. And you can't make a coherent poem out of that either. Which is why the storyboard is a helpful exercise.

A poem like 'I Cannot Remember My Mother' or 'It Ain't What You Do, It's What It Does to You' does not announce its speaker in the same way as 'My Blue Hen': its images are not framed in a dramatic scene. We assume the speaker is simply a poet reflecting somewhere, probably at their desk. It's still worth thinking what a storyboard would look like for these sorts of poems, though. The speaker still needs to be intelligible, and to move coherently through images so we can trust them to guide us on the journey. Or to put it another way: even if your video opens and closes on just a face, it needs to be the same face, perhaps a little closer.

Defeating Your Inner Policeman

As you write about other people, or address them in letters, you may well find yourself haunted and inhibited by the fears of what they might think if they read it, or – often even more so – what other people, such as your parents, might feel if it were published. You might find yourself dwelling on stories in the press where families are torn apart by revelations in books, and before you know it, you will have constructed yourself an 'inner policeman', which is what Ted Hughes called the figures in our minds that stop us writing.

Like real policemen, inner ones can be there for good reasons. It is wrong to say cruel and untrue things in print, or send a poison-pen letter, and policemen are right to remind you of that. The problems come when your policemen grow too large, and you can't write anything at all because their 'no' is all you can hear. A head is not a very big space, after all.

If you are stuck with an overgrown, shouty, inner policeman then you need to get him under control. Identifying and naming him can help with this – try to think about who exactly might be hurt by your writing and why you think that. Are you being fair on them? Wouldn't they really want you to write? And if they wouldn't, why not? Are they being fair on you?

Then remind yourself that writing a poem and publishing it are two very different things, and that publishing a poem to a national readership and widespread ejaculations of shock over the breakfast pancakes is a different thing still. In fact, that hasn't happened since Ted Hughes published *Birthday Letters*, and it is really not likely to happen to you.

Writing for yourself can never do any harm, because no one has to see it. It cannot travel on its own from your computer to your mother's Facebook page or your father's newspaper or your ex-lover's letterbox. You are in charge, and you can choose when and if and how to share your poems. Publishing is also in the future and you can make a careful, ethical decision when it becomes a real prospect. For now, write your poem. You might be surprised how loving it is, and, if you ever do show it to its subject, how much they like it. People like to be seen as much as praised, very often. Remember, a poem is your best attention, and you are giving it to them.

ROOM TO WRITE
Private Space

Once you have made your poetry palace, you should defend it
carefully. This means thinking about your privacy rules, and what
suits you. Do you want to have your writing as a secret? In which
case, put your poetry shelf somewhere inconspicuous, put a code
word on your poetry folder on your laptop, and draw the curtain
round your desk. When you book yourself poetry time in your
diary you might need to create a regular excuse for your family and
friends – an exercise class or a work meeting.

Or would you prefer to have some backup in your commitment to
writing? If so, you could tell your friends and family that writing is
what you are doing and your time and space are important. Use
the act of telling to reinforce your boundaries, and your sense of
your work's importance.

Either way, keep giving yourself the time and space to write. If you
don't make the room, the poems can't arrive.

5

FINDING YOUR SOUND

Of all the technical aspects of poetry, the use of sound is perhaps the most wrapped in jargon and fable. This is partly because describing the sound of words in other words is extremely hard work. In a poem, rhythm, rhyme, assonance and onomatopoeia can all work together in a single line or even a single word, but to explain how this happens and why it works in literary critical terms requires separating and naming the elements: the labour of many sentences.

It is a finicky activity, too, and not one that many people enjoy. When I go into schools as a poet, one of the questions I am often, resentfully, asked is: 'Did you put all the rhythms and things in on purpose?' The students have been taught some labels for the sounds of verse, how to spell 'onomatopoeia' and 'pentameter', and told to include them in the fourth paragraph of their essay, in a secondary position to 'theme'. As a result, they now perceive sounds either as fiendishly difficult crossword clues waiting to be solved, or as decorations, sprinkles on the cake of a poem.

But, though analysing sound in verse is ponderous and hard, creating it is instinctive and almost alarmingly easy. The same school students who questioned my rhythms would, if asked to write in response to a poem they liked, echo the rhythm without even thinking about it; and probably the assonance and alliteration too, just as you, while responding to poems in this book, will certainly have written with sound. Sounds in poems are primary, not secondary; they arrive with the images. They are the cake, not the decoration.

Paradoxically, the people most highly trained in feature-spotting – English professors and literary critics – may well find it harder to create their own tune; while the most natural sound producers – small children, students new to a language and people with dyslexia – often find it hardest to label what they have done. The two groups – instinctive poets and counter-intuitive critics – naturally resent each other. Worse, your own inner critic and inner poet may well not get on at all.

But in order to advance your writing process and write your own poem, your inner critic will have to talk to your inner poet. You are all ready to create sound, but in order to tame that ability and get it to work for you – tune it up, trim it, cut it to fit – you will also have to hear it, control it and sometimes name it. You will need to be confident so that you can create your own tune, a way of putting the sounds and words together that does not belong to anyone else. The following poems help you to focus on doing that.

Your Sound:
'I Come From'

To start with, a rhythm so strong it has its own international project.

George Ella Lyon's Where I'm From project is freely available on the internet, and thousands of people have used it. Simply, it invites you to write a poem from a model originally by Lyon. This might sound unpromising, but her poem is so strong that it has the magical effect of making every reader want to write their own version, and so simple that they can. All it does is list the sounds, sights and objects of home with a marvellous rhythm as a link.

Robert Seatter's version is an English one. The poem may be especially evocative if you were raised in the seventies – but names such as *Look and Learn* are still resonant if you weren't – they have been woven into an incantation, a magic spell.

I Come From

I come from a suburb waiting forever
for the train to London,
from smashed windows, graffiti,
fog on the platform,
skinheads and fights
if you look the wrong way
I come from clean handkerchiefs,
dinner money, God,
please and *sorry* one hundred times over,
draft excluders and double glazing
I come from *Chambers Etymological Dictionary*,
maths tables, 11+, *Look & Learn*,
an almost complete set of *Observer I-Spy* books,
a family of teachers and yet more teachers,
an Orkney grandfather, a Shropshire grandma,
from no accent at all
I come from kindness

I come from doh-re-me: *The Sound of Music*
recorders, clarinets, a pianola
all the way from Scotland
I come from rats behind the garage,
and a man who followed me
back from the library
I come from silence
I come from a garden
from my father mowing the lawn into the dark,
from fences, walls, gates and hedges,
Cuthbert's seed packets, *The Perfect Small Garden*
from the sound through the night
of trains, trains, trains.

Robert Seatter

Azfa Awad is Tanzanian British. She read Robert Seatter's poem and answered it with her own version. Hers is a very different experience and a very different collection of stuff, but it's still the rhythm and the concrete images – 'the manky dishes' and 'damp, brown smell' – that root her metaphors and allow the poem to take flight.

I Come From . . .

I come from the streets
That replaced grass and flowers
With concrete and syringes;

I come from grey flats towering
Injecting venom into the sky's blue skin.

I come from salty tears
Running down his stubbled chin,
Gorilla hands
Stained from building car parts –
Factory work –
The One-Way Ticket to a better future.

I come from
Manky dishes
Stained mattresses
White walls dripping
With the damp, brown
Smell of poverty.

I come from school:
The education system
That gives me a pen
Only to poke myself blind with,

I come from insanity:
From catching falling stars
Born of the pregnant night:
Aflame with dreams and poetry.

Azfa Awad (eighteen)

Your Turn

Let yourself write you own 'I come from' poem.

How you sound is intimately connected with where you come from. Focus on your images and the sound will arrive.

Think of your home – the place that seems home to you.

It may not be the place that other people say is home.

You may have left it when you were very young.

Start with lists of three – always a magic number.

And the five senses.

And the rhythmic incantation: I come from.

I come from: three tastes of your home. Curry, toast, tea.

I come from: three smells of your home. Food, ironing, gardens.

I come from: three sounds of your home. Accents, music, the outside.

I come from: three textures or feelings of your home. Heavy curtains, cool air conditioning, warm beds.

I come from: objects. Three books, three bits of furniture, three things that were on the table.

People: the people that were there, the people that weren't.

Fears: real and unreal.

Joys.

And something bigger for an ending.

Three skies.

Three bits of weather.

The thing that was going to take you away. (Dreams and poetry. Trains, trains, trains.)

Now write up your list, remembering your best list rules: changes of tone, light and shade, starting small and concrete if you want to end big and abstract.

Read it aloud. This poem will certainly have a rhythm, so listen to it and clarify it. If you've put words in an order that gets in the way of the rhythm – the *poverty smell, damp and brown*, instead of the *damp, brown smell of poverty* – then sort it out. You're finding your own rhythm.

In General: Finding Your Own Rhythm

We all speak in rhythm. The rhythm of our own language is one of the primary things we learn – babies babble in it long before they can speak – and one of its primary qualities. All languages have their own dominant rhythm. For instance, English and Swedish are similar languages, but English usually emphasizes the second syllable of a word, and has a limping or iambic tune, while Swedish usually emphasizes the first syllable, so it has a trochaic tune. If you play an old-fashioned English video backwards it sounds like Swedish. Knowing our own language-tune doesn't mean we can't learn other rhythms – we do that all the time, especially when we like something. Imitation, mostly of *Neighbours* and *Home and Away*, is how Australian 'upspeak' spread irritatingly through the UK, for instance. Hearing and echoing speech-rhythm is a conversational, primary, intuitive, human thing to do.

That's why rhythm is also one of the most transferable aspects of poetry. Anyone who has written a 'little wasp' poem or an 'I come from' poem will have imitated the source poems' rhythms because it's almost impossible not to. It's also quite easy, for most poets, to hear when a rhythm is running smoothly and when it falters or breaks. Talking *about* rhythm, on the other hand, and explaining *why* something sounds wrong, is not easy at all. In fact, for most readers, counting beats and marking metre is one of the hardest aspects of verse-analysis to learn. This is partly because it's slippery and irregular: rhythm in English verse is based on stresses (the syllable of a word you emphasize) and these vary between accents, areas and speakers – think of the different ways a Glaswegian, a Jamaican British person and a London barrister might pronounce the word 'understand', for instance. But it is also because it is a counter-intuitive thing to do, and clumsy too: the description of why a rhythm works is always much less graceful than the example.

If you want to look up the labels of English verse, you will find they are widely available on the internet. But please don't feel you need to. You can make rhythms, listen to rhythms, and edit for rhythm without counting or naming feet. You will learn more, as a poet, by noticing great bits of rhythm in poems, and reading them aloud or just letting them live and echo in your head than you will by quantifying them. When you get to the point of wanting to explain precisely what is happening in a bit of rhythm, then you will also have found precisely the right time to look up the meta-language and understand it easily. In the meantime, in your own work, listen for your own rhythm.

Faster and Greener:
Sounds of the Summer

Some readers and writers take refuge from the endless difficulties of counting feet (which are not the kind you walk on, but units of stress) in the easier pursuit of numbering syllables, for example counting out the seventeen syllables of a haiku. Poems created in patterns like this are said to be in *syllabic verse*.

Personally, I have never seen the point, because rhythms sing, or don't, through an English haiku whether or not it has seventeen syllables. But if these numbers and shapes help you write your own poem, then please, go right ahead. Dylan Thomas did, and it worked out fine, though you may notice that in fact the lilting rhythm is often one of the strongest features of his poems, rather than the syllable count, which you can't hear at all.

Now as I was young and easy under the apple boughs
About the lilting house and happy as the grass was green,
  The night above the dingle starry,
    Time let me hail and climb
  Golden in the heydays of his eyes.

For instance.

The same rhythm drives
this extraordinary poem
by Frank O'Hara. The
rhythm breaks – brilliantly
– on 'O you'.

Animals

Have you forgotten what we were like then
when we were still first rate
and the day came fat with an apple in its mouth

it's no use worrying about Time
but we did have a few tricks up our sleeves
and turned some sharp corners

the whole pasture looked like our meal
we didn't need speedometers
we could manage cocktails out of ice and water

I wouldn't want to be faster
or greener than now if you were with me O you
were the best of all my days

Frank O'Hara

Your Turn

The rhythm of these poems is easy to catch, and so is the golden, natural imagery, childlike diction, and bitter-sweet nostalgia.

—

Try it.

—

Your poem begins:

Have you forgotten?

It takes you back to a bright field in your mind.

When you were young and easy.

Aim for that mixed-up, non-grammatical, childlike voice,

When the day came . . .

When the night was . . .

And the sun . . .

And the pastures . . .

And the streams . . .

Let Time the abstraction do something in your poem.

And Time let me . . .

It's no use worrying about Time.

End with an 'O'.

O you, O then . . .

—

As you write up your poem, you will notice that you have caught the Thomas/O'Hara rhythm. Try noticing the other sounds too. Which vowel are you repeating? It may well be an 'o', echoing the source poems. You may well be echoing the sibilants – repeated 's' of the source poems too. But there may be something else, as well – a pattern of sound, a half-rhyme, an off rhythm – that is not in the source poem. That is your sound. Listen to it.

In General: Where Your Rhythm Breaks

When you have written a poem in a particular rhythm and are
going back over it, editing for sound, you may notice that you have
broken the rhythm in certain places. It's tempting to tidy these up
– but not necessarily the best idea. Rhythm breaks or changes with
the thought of the poem, and sometimes the places where they
break are the best parts of a poem. If you look back at 'Animals',
for example, you will see that the rhythm breaks on 'O' – and that's
a beautiful thing.

Finding Your Local Soundscape:
'On This Island'

The poet W. H. Auden was very interested in Old English verse, especially when he was a young poet. Poems such as *Beowulf* are written to a different set of rules than, say, Shakespeare's sonnets. Shakespeare rhymed, like his French contemporaries, and he used an Italian form, the sonnet. But Old English verse doesn't try to rhyme. Instead, it alliterates – it repeats the same letter or sound many times in one line. Sometimes, this sound is a vowel, which is called assonance. Assonance and alliteration are more frequent in English than full rhyme, so the resulting sound can be more natural – avoiding poetic inversion and convolutions in order to land on the right word – while also heightening and brightening sound.

Auden's 'On This Island' is a poem about a southern English landscape that is packed with these heightened English sounds. Reading it and responding to it is a good way of heightening and brightening your own sounds, and the sound of your particular English. In case this sounds mystical or unconvincing, I've followed Auden's poem with two responses to it written in a single lunch hour by schoolgirls who did not have English as a first language. Their mother tongues and their home landscapes sing through their poems, and yours can too. As Auden knew, the glory of English is the many languages which make it up, and the huge variety of vocabulary and sound that jostle with in. English is poor in perfect rhyme, but rich in vocabulary and soundscapes. One of them is yours.

'On This Island' isn't written in an alliterative metre, but it is influenced by it. As well as alliteration and assonance, it also uses a lot of half-rhyme and internal rhyme – rhymes inside the line – which echoes Old English verse. You won't notice all that if you read it aloud, though: what you will notice is the onomatopoeia. This is a poem that sounds uncannily like the sea swaying on a pebbly beach.

On This Island

Look, stranger, on this island now
The leaping light for your delight discovers,
Stand stable here
And silent be,
That through the channels of the ear
May wander like a river
The swaying sound of the sea.

Here at a small field's ending pause
Where the chalk wall falls to the foam and its tall ledges
Oppose the pluck
And knock of the tide,
And the shingle scrambles after the suck-
ing surf, and a gull lodges
A moment on its sheer side.

Far off like floating seeds the ships
Diverge on urgent voluntary errands,
And this full view
Indeed may enter
And move in memory as now these clouds do,
That pass the harbour mirror
And all the summer through the water saunter.

W. H. Auden

Rukiya came to the UK from Bangladesh when she was six. Her poem shows us a child's-eye view of the jungle, and her sounds, with their strong sibilants and open vowels, echo the tune of Bengali English.

Sylhet

There,
Sun birds chipper,
Their feathers, light lime,
Seep in the sunshine.

Crisp leaves grow,
Wild and olive,
And the silent streams,
Run,

Fresh water,
To guide the ilish
Silver, simple fish,
Away to the sea.

Mango trees
Summit and soar,
Stalk high above
The forest floor.

Where
A Bengal tiger,
Obsolete
As an emperor

Trembles
As the hushed wind-
Breathes –

Rukiya Khatun (seventeen)

Vivien had left Hungary
just two years before she
wrote this poem. The
Hungarian wind sounds
through the open vowels.

Look stranger,

on these flat lands
now.
Before you, endless sky
fills empty space.
Stand here,
and open up your mind.
Notice the light
riding on its cloud horse
throwing shadows
on the grassy ground.
Stand here
and hear the whistle of the wind
blowing the golden sand.
Remember it,
the free and wild wind,

as a gentle touch.

Vivien Urban (fourteen)

Your Turn

Neither Rukiya nor Vivien were even English A-Level students when they wrote their poems. Nor were they explicitly thinking about sound: they were thinking about the Auden poem and their own home landscape. The sounds followed naturally, or came by poetry magic, whichever you prefer.

Find your own sound. Try this spell for yourself.

Read 'On This Island' aloud, at least three times.

Think of your own home landscape: a view you love, that you can conjure easily in your mind's eye.

Make it a perfect day for this place, the perfect weather.

Where is the very best spot to see this view?

Guide us there.

It's important that we see it, so use the imperative mood – commands.

Look stranger –

See . . .

Stand . . .

Breathe . . .

Feel . . .

Now we are at the perfect spot – what will we see?

Remember your other senses: smell, taste, hearing, touch

What should we notice?

Show us something moving.

Something still.

Something far.

Something near.

And what will this picture do in our minds, later?

—

Put your poem away for a day or two.

When you come back, read it aloud and listen to your own sound.

Think about making it louder and clearer.

Rewrite, and read aloud again. What are the letters *you* keep repeating?

Which vowels sound though *your* poem?

What do *you* like to rhyme?

That's a soundscape: yours.

In General: Punctuation: Poetry Percussion

Some poems, like Fatimah Asghar's, coming up next, abandon punctuation to get a rushing, headlong, breathless feeling.

It's an attractive effect. So attractive, that many beginning poets go through a phase of also giving up on punctuation. Text without stops is quick and easy to write and says 'poem' very clearly – a bit like reaching for the 'centre' button on the word processor. Most published contemporary poets, though, don't just use conventional punctuation at all times, but are quite obsessed with it.

That's because punctuation is a store of sound effects – breaths, pauses, drops of the voice. It makes a difference to the tone of a poem if you use italics instead of speech marks, and the pace if you put in a semicolon over a comma. Punctuation is a drum kit – and poems without it are sometimes just a little less rich.

Punctuation is your choice, but make sure you've made it thoughtfully. One good exercise for almost all poems is to write the poem out as prose at the drafting stage, and check that your punctuation is the way you want it before winding the poem back round its line breaks.

Calling in Your People

Build on your sounds and rhythms by using this rich and generous poem by Pakistani/Kashmiri/ American Fatimah Asghar. It builds in turn on the famous poem by Martin Niemoller, written during the Nazis' rise to power.

First they came for the socialists, and I did not speak out—

   Because I was not a socialist.

Then they came for the trade unionists, and I did not speak out—

   Because I was not a trade unionist.

Then they came for the Jews, and I did not speak out—

If They Should Come for Us

these are my people & I find
them on the street & shadow
through any wild all wild
my people my people
a dance of strangers in my blood
the old woman's sari dissolving to wind
bindi a new moon on her forehead
I claim her my kin & sew
the star of her to my breast
the toddler dangling from stroller
hair a fountain of dandelion seed
at the bakery I claim them too
the sikh uncle at the airport
who apologizes for the pat
down the muslim man who abandons
his car at the traffic light drops
to his knees at the call of the azan
& the muslim man who sips
good whiskey at the start of maghrib
the lone khala at the park
pairing her kurta with crocs
my people my people I can't be lost
when I see you my compass
is brown & gold & blood
my compass a muslim teenage
snapback & high-tops gracing
the subway platform

Because I was not a
Jew.

Then they came for me—
and there was no one left
to speak for me.

mashallah I claim them all
my country is made
in my people's image
if they come for you they
come for me too in the dead
of winter a flock of
aunties step out on the sand
their dupattas turn to ocean
a colony of uncles grind their palms
& a thousand jasmines bell the air
my people I follow you like constellations
we hear the glass smashing the street
& the nights opening their dark
our names this country's wood
for the fire my people my people
the long years we've survived the long
years yet to come I see you map
my sky the light your lantern long
ahead & I follow I follow

Fatimah Asghar

Your Turn

Who are your people?

Write a series of ampersands (&) down the side of a piece of A4.

Beside each one, write a snapshot image of someone you consider
yours

the toddler dangling from stroller
hair a fountain of dandelion seed
at the bakery I claim them too
the sikh uncle at the airport
who apologizes for the pat
down the muslim man who abandons
his car at the traffic light drops
to his knees at the call of the azan
& the muslim man who sips
good whiskey at the start of maghrib
the lone khala at the park
pairing her kurta with crocs

Keep going all the way to the bottom of the page.

Now look at your list.

Where is your ending and beginning?

Join them with 'I claim them' and 'my people my people' if you
like – or think of a phrase of your own.

Think about ordering your list.

Remember the rules of contrast, light and shade, of starting with the general and ending with the particular.

You might want to break those rules here, and use a rhetorical flourish.

You can borrow 'I follow I follow' as an ending if you like.

This poem might take some time to get right. Keep it in your notebook or on your screen and add to it every so often.

Listen carefully to the sounds and rhythm coming through – they're yours.

Sounding Right

You won't call in your sound without calling in your landscape, your language and your people. As you do so, you may well find yourself stuck or anxious, because fears about race, class and gender are some of the biggest and most muscly inner policemen.

For instance, I didn't write any poems till I was twenty-seven because, even though I was middle class, white and very educated, I didn't feel I could because I was a woman. I wanted to be the object of a poem, not the writer. I knew lots of women novelists, but the only woman poet I knew was Sylvia Plath, and while I admired and admire her work, I've never loved it or identified with it. Also, her life story as told to me strongly implied that poetry drove women mad.

So I only started to write poetry when I started to read women poets: Carol Ann Duffy, Selima Hill, Grace Nichols and Sharon Olds were the earliest figures in my pantheon but I have added hundreds since. They recorded experiences I recognized as mine. I saw myself in their work. And that let me join in.

If you want to write poems, you need to see yourself in other poems, and if you are a woman, or of colour, or gay, or d/Deaf or disabled or in fact from any group that isn't very privileged heterosexual young white men (and even then . . .) you need to seek out and read poems where you can see that identity represented and where you can hear voices like your own. There is nothing silly, or old-fashioned, or politically correct, or corny, or self-indulgent, or cliched about this: it's just a need that all writers have.

So if your poem sounds wrong, if you are stuck for a subject, if you find yourself hesitating to write your own experience because there seems to be something 'not worthy' about it, take a moment to think why that might be. Then go and read some poems by one of your people – a poet who writes about experience like yours in a way you admire. Borrow their courage. Make it yours.

Listen Out

As you start to explore contemporary poetry, you may well find that you are listening to and watching videos on the internet almost as much as you are reading. Don't worry. The distinction between 'page' poets and 'performance' poets is breaking down rapidly. Now we just have poets, with work available in several formats.

As you read and listen, and find favourites, you'll probably also find notices for poets' readings in bookshops and theatres. Try to go. Listening to a good poet read live can be a truly wonderful experience, opening new dimensions in their work. Even listening to a bad poet can be creatively excruciating, because the experience sparks words in your mind and opens you up to the conversation of poetry.

You might also find advertisements for local poetry slams or open mikes, where anyone can bring a poem and read it aloud. Again, go along and listen. Give yourself permission to be an audience member, to love and hate what you hear. Maybe one day you'll want to join in.

6 THE WHITE SPACE

Time Travel

Form and Shape:
Time and Space

Form sits next to sound in poetry's hierarchy of difficulty, high up in the locked cupboard of things that other people know.

Form meaning shape: shape in the world of sound, rhyme connected to rhyme; inherited shape, passed generation to generation; and shape on the page, where the inked words go on the white space.

This chapter focuses on the white space and sets out to show you that placing words upon it is not as hard as all that, and can even be fun.

You will need two (not very) technical terms.

Line break – the place where you end a line to go on to the next one.

Stanza break – the place where you end a stanza (a verse) and move, through a wider space, on to the next one.

When you are following a traditional form, the places where you break the lines and stanzas are determined for you: it's where the last beat or rhyme falls. When you aren't following a form though, it's harder.

Is it a breath? Or a pause? People often say so – but they say the same about commas, so how does that work? Should your line breaks be in the same place as your commas? Are some poems full of gasps?

I find it more helpful to think of the white space as time and space.

Let's start with time.

Writing Slo-Mo

This poem uses the white space primarily as time, slowing the action down until we can see the cricket ball being caught in a hand – though the poem does gesture at the arc of a ball too. The metaphor of the apple makes it feel as if it took all summer.

The Catch

Forget
the long, smouldering
afternoon. It is

this moment
when the ball scoots
off the edge

of the bat; upwards,
backwards, falling
seemingly

beyond him
yet he reaches
and picks it

out
of its loop
like

an apple
from a branch,
the first of the season.

Simon Armitage

Your Turn

Try using the white space to slow down the action in your own poem.

Think of a scene which happens slowly in your imagination. Choose a bodily, perhaps sporting one: diving into water, connecting with a ball at football or tennis. Or just a vivid one: the moment of an accident, the moment news is given . . .

Try to think of the white space as resistant, heavy, something that you are pushing against or forging a path through.

It is this moment . . .

Detail it in just a few spare images . . .

Try laying it out down the page using lots of space. Maybe one or two words to the line . . .

You'll need a satisfying metaphor to close.

Line Breaks and Breath

Some poets say that a line break is a breath, a natural break, and that certainly can be one of its effects. If you end a line with a punctuation break and a line break and perhaps a rhyme as well, you will make a breath in your poem. (This is called end-stopping, because everything stops at the end.)

It can be more interesting, though, to pit these things against each other – so your lines spill over their own edges and don't let you breathe out, like in the Fatimah Asghar poem, or so the line breaks make you hold your breath in wonder, as in this poem.

A Blessing

Just off the highway to Rochester, Minnesota,
Twilight bounds softly forth on the grass.
And the eyes of those two Indian ponies
Darken with kindness.
They have come gladly out of the willows
To welcome my friend and me.
We step over the barbed wire into the pasture
Where they have been grazing all day, alone.
They ripple tensely, they can hardly contain their happiness
That we have come.
They bow shyly as wet swans. They love each other.
There is no loneliness like theirs.
At home once more,
They begin munching the young tufts of spring in the darkness.
I would like to hold the slenderer one in my arms,
For she has walked over to me
And nuzzled my left hand.
She is black and white,
Her mane falls wild on her forehead,
And the light breeze moves me to caress her long ear
That is delicate as the skin over a girl's wrist.
Suddenly I realize
That if I stepped out of my body I would break
Into blossom.

James Wright

Your Turn

One of the many beautiful things about 'A Blessing' is that it seems artless: as if it were just a speech act, thrown on the paper as easily as it was spoken. But in fact almost every line break is doing some work to hold the poem close to the magical moment of communion with the horses. Look at that tenth line, for instance: 'That we have come'. It hasn't just fallen off the line before – it was pushed over by the horses' brimming happiness. The line itself is short because the horses have a modest pause before the next line and also to create a shape like a bowing swan, or horse.

Take 'The Blessing' Challenge:

Type the poem up without line breaks (it is available on the internet, if that helps).

Then, without looking at the original, put in the line breaks for yourself, thinking out each one.

Ask yourself – where am I moving forward here, in time and space?

What word do I want at the end of the line?

And at the beginning?

And where should the reader breathe?

Or not breathe?

When you have got to the end, and made it as satisfying as you can, have a look at your version next to the original.

What have you lost, and what have you gained?

Think of this as a sort of barre exercise.

You're building a muscle memory of line breaks.

In General: Edge Words

The word at the end of each line

and the word at the

beginning of the line.

get a bit more space.

and push against

space. So

they are worth thinking about.

A verb will give more space to the action as it pushes

into the white spaces

An adjective will pull us over into its special

noun below.

Connectives – *and, also* – will whizz us, smartly and

quickly to the next line.

An 'I'

at the end of a line leaves your speaker facing out into the world

Little words which are normally attached to other words – articles
like *a*

and *the* –

on the end of

a line might look a

bit small and lonely –

On the other hand, Sharon Olds uses them there all the time . . .

Time Travel:
The Stanza Break

The poems of the great American poet Sharon Olds very often tumble out as a single utterance, sprinting to the bottom of the page through inimitably strange line breaks. This poem, though, takes us through time and space in a wonderfully clear, imitable way.

Each stanza is like a different shot in a small film. Each line moves us a steady step forward.

Time-Travel

I have learned to go back and walk around
and find the windows and doors. Outside
it is hot, the pines are black, the lake
laps. It is 1955 and I am
looking for my father.
I walk from a small room to a big one
through a doorway. The walls and floors are pine,
full of splinters. I come upon him.

I can possess him like this, the funnies
rising and falling on his big stomach,
his big solid secret body
where he puts the bourbon.
He belongs to me forever like this,
the red plaid shirt, the baggy pants,
the long perfectly turned legs,
the soft padded hands folded across his body,
the hair dark as a burnt match,
the domed, round eyes closed,
the firm mouth. Sleeping it off
in the last summer the family was together.

I have learned to walk
so quietly into that summer
no one knows I am there. He rests
easy as a baby. Upstairs
mother weeps. Out in the tent

my brother reads my diary. My sister
is changing boyfriends somewhere in a car
and down by the shore of the lake there is a girl
twelve years old, watching the water
fold and disappear. I walk up behind her,
I touch her shoulder, she turns her head –

I see my face. She looks through me
up at the house. This is the one I have
come for. I gaze in her eyes, the waves
thick as the air in hell, curling in
over and over. She does not know
any of this will ever stop.
She does not know she is the one

survivor.

Sharon Olds

Your Turn

Think of a time in your past you remember clearly, that you can revisit as Sharon Olds revisits her holiday house. Remember it fully, using your five senses. Jot down the images.

Use Sharon Olds's stanza openings to write about it:

—

I have learned to go back . . .

I can possess . . .

I have learned to walk . . .

I see my face . . .

—

If you like, you could use the last word of the poem to travel far forwards in time, even to the present, as Sharon Olds does with the word 'survivor'.

In General: What Track is Your Poem Making?

It often helps me to think of the white space as enormous.

As all of time and all of space.

Infinitely big, and very cold.

My sentence is my moon buggy across an endless frost.

What pattern do I want to make?

A thin,

      solitary

            path

                  across

                        aeons of time?

Or do I want to pack the land with loud rows of warm sound?

Stanzas are bigger units of time.

I at the end of a stanza can take a leap across time.

(It's lonely here on) Couplet Island

Last year, this year: as the
seasons turn, we all sit
and make comparisons.
This translation of the
poet Rumi (a free-verse
version of a Persian ode)
shows him playing the
Furniture Game with the
idea. The images are
brilliant, but spare a
moment to think about
the shape, too.

The poet is adrift in time
and space, swirling in a
vast wine glass. His
central image is the
moon, reflecting in a
pool. As he despairs, he
looks around, and sees
blossom. The shape of
the lines reflected all that.
The first three stanzas are
two-line couplets which

Burnt Kabob

Last year, I admired wines. This,
I'm wandering inside the red world.

Last year, I gazed at the fire.
This year I'm burnt kabob.

Thirst drove me down to the water
where I drank the moon's reflection.

Now I am a lion staring up totally
lost in love with the thing itself.

Don't ask questions about longing.
Look in my face.

Soul drunk, body ruined, these two
sit helpless in a wrecked wagon.
Neither knows how to fix it.

And my heart, I'd say it was more
like a donkey sunk in a mudhole,
struggling and miring deeper.

each portray a pair of reflections: this year/last year, moon/reflection, lion/moon. Each of these couplets is isolated, as the poet, lion and moon are, on the page as in time and space. As he starts to come back down to earth – the sink hole – his stanzas get slightly longer, and the last one is snagged in four lines of blossom.

God, of course, is on his own.

But listen to me: for one moment, quit being sad. Hear blessings dropping their blossoms around you. God.

Rumi, rendering by Coleman Barks

Your Turn

Try a *this year, last year* poem for yourself.

Where were you this time last year?

How are you doing? Better or worse?

Remember your Furniture Game prompts, and run through them, making the comparison.

Last year I held a thin teacup . . .

This year I'm the teabag . . .

—

Last year, I patted a Pomeranian

This year, I'm on the lead.

—

My soul . . .

My heart is . . .

—

Remember all your rules about contrast, plots and voltas – Rumi has a beautiful little turn in stanza four.

—

As you write up, use the white space to express your movement across time. It might be an archipelago of couplets, or some larger islands, or even a peninsula with a rock at the end.

A Glass of Tea

(after Rumi)

Last year, I held a glass of tea to the light. This year,
I swirl like a tealeaf in the streets of Oxford.

Last year, I stared into navy blue sky. This year,
I am roaming under colourless clouds.

Last year, I watched the dazzling sun dance gracefully.
   This year, the faint sun moves futurelessly.

Migration drove me down this bumpy road,
Where I fell and smelt the soil, where I arose and sensed
   the cloud.

Now I am a bird, flying in the breeze,
Lost over the alien earth.

Don't stop and ask me questions.
Look into my eyes and feel my heart.

It is bruised, aching and sore.
My eyes are veiled with onion skin.

I sit helplessly in an injured nest,
Not knowing how to fix it.

And my heart, I'd say
Is displaced

Struggling to find its place.

Shukria Rezaei (seventeen)

Couplet Island 2

This is another poem about being isolated in time and space – in this case in an abusive relationship. The couple are frozen in (grand, biblical, commanding) couplets on the page.

In That Year

And in that year my body was a pillar of smoke
and even his hands could not hold me.

And in that year my mind was an empty table
and he laid his thoughts down like dishes of plenty.

And in that year my heart was the old monument,
the folly, and no use could be found for it.

And in that year my tongue spoke the language
of insects and not even my father knew me.

And in that year I waited for the horses
but they only shifted their feet in the darkness.

And in that year I imagined a vain thing;
I believed that the world would come for me.

And in that year I gave up on all the things
I was promised and left myself to sadness.

And then that year lay down like a path
and I walked it, I walked it, I walk it.

Kim Moore

This is a wonderful poem to imitate, biblical diction and all.

Remember your Furniture Game prompts, think of a particular year in your life, and start

And in that year my body . . .

And in that year my mind . . .

And in that year my words . . .

And in that year . . .

—

This is a poem about time, so make sure the shape of your poem echoes that.

You could use isolated couplets like Kim Moore, but if you are writing about rich, warm, interconnected experiences you should use longer, more interconnected lines.

In General: Capital Letters

Unless they are writing formal rhymed verse, and want to signal that they are doing so, or unless grammar requires it, contemporary poets don't use capital letters at the beginnings of lines.

You may as well follow this convention. It's important if you are submitting to a magazine, and anyway, the more poetry you read, the noisier capital letters will come to seem.

Unfortunately, no one told Microsoft about contemporary poetry, and Word will keep trying to insert them for you.

Time Travel Boxes:
Regular Stanzas

In the Sharon Olds poem, the stanzas function like paragraphs –
when the subject of the poem moves forward and back in time, she
takes a new stanza. Her stanzas are, in poetry terms, *free* – they
have different irregular numbers of lines. This is very fitting for a
poem making free with time.

Stanzas with a set number of lines – six, five, four – are not free,
but formal. This gives you a different set of effects because the
rules of the stanza are working against the rules of natural
paragraphing.

My Beast

When I was a child I worried
that when I got my chance to love a beast
I would not be up to the task and I'd fail.

As he came in for the kiss I'd turn away
or gag on the mane in my mouth
and the fair-haired prince
and the dress that Beauty wore
on the last page of my Ladybird book
would be lost to me forever.

But now I see that the last thing my father
driving home late from work
would have on his mind is the gardens
flashing past and he would never stop

In 'My Beast', the stanza breaks move us forward and back in time, just like in the Sharon Olds poem. But the square stanzas are also like the pages of a book being turned, with a different picture on each, and also trap us in a regular shape which – as this poem is as much about confinement and turning the pages of a picture book, as well as about moving forward and backward in time – works brilliantly.

to pick a rose for one of his daughters
and if some misfortune such as

his Volvo reversing into a beast's carriage
did occur and I ended up at the castle
as compensation, the beast would probably
just set me to work cleaning and I'd never
look up from scrubbing a floor and catch him
in the doorway admiring my technique.

Still, as I've heard my dad say,
he and his children may not always
be brilliant but they always turn up,
and in time when the beast comes to realise
that I haven't tried to escape
he'll give me leave one Sunday a month

to visit my family and access
to his vast library and in bed at night
reading by the light of a candle
I'd shut another calf-bound volume
and hear its quality thud
with something like happiness.

Lorraine Mariner

Your Turn

What did you worry about, when you were a child?

And what did you dream of?

How were these dreams mixed in with films and books?

What item in a book did you most covet?

What was your secret dream?

Try to be very concrete with your images –

When the three-wish fairy came, what were you going to ask for?

What dress were you going to have?

When you went on your quest, what was going to be in your knapsack?

—

Borrow some of Mariner's openings to structure your thoughts. The volta in 'But now I see' is especially important.

—

When I was a child I worried . . .

—

When I got my chance . . .

—

But now I see . . .

—

And in time . . .

—

When you write up your poem, try the effect of regular stanzas.
Choose a number of lines – three, four, six – that fits the first few
sentences, and try keeping to that pattern throughout the poem,
while also remembering that line breaks and stanza breaks are
time and space. You might have to move things around. You might
have to change the number of lines. And back again. If it's hard
work, keep at it. This will do you good.

In General: Find a Rule from Inside Your Poem

The shape of a poem, like the sound of a poem, is integral to the poem – you will almost always have some idea, from the very first, of whether your poem is long or short, wide or narrow, curved or square.

You will quickly develop, too, an idea of whether it has some sort of regular pattern to it – if you want it to have a formal, restricted feeling or to range freely, mastering the page.

If you do want it to have a regular pattern, but aren't sure what, don't impose one from outside – look for the pattern in your draft.

What length is your best line? Try taking that as a regular line length.

What pattern is your best stanza? Couplet, threes, fours?

How would that work throughout your poem?

What does a rule like that do to time in your poem?

Experiment freely – it's fun, the best way to learn, and the best way to find your own form and your own poem.

Remember, you can drop a line or two at the end of the poem to make a closing couplet or striking last line.

Very often, you will find yourself using traditional English verse lines – iambic limping beats, five of them to a line, like Shakespeare. This is because our national verse is based on our natural language, and because you are joining a conversation in it and about it. And because you are brilliant, of course.

The Segue:
Like This

The future is a very big white space. So is the realm of the conditional – what would be. But a poem can go there. In fact, once you have mastered the stanza break, a poem can segue effortlessly between the future/conditional and the present as easily as any film. Look at these segues, created seven hundred years ago by the poet Rumi. Each 'like this' returns us to the speaker and his lover, moving together in an embrace.

If anyone asks you

how the perfect satisfaction
of all our sexual wanting
will look, lift your face
and say,

Like this.

When someone mentions the gracefulness
of the night sky, climb up on the roof
and dance and say,

Like this.

If anyone wants to know what 'spirit' is,
or what 'God's fragrance' means,
lean your head toward him or her.
Keep your face there close.

Like this.

When someone quotes the old poetic image
about clouds gradually uncovering the moon,
slowly loosen knot by knot the strings
of your robe.

Like this.

If anyone wonders how Jesus raised the dead,
don't try to explain the miracle.
Kiss me on the lips.

Like this. Like this.

When someone asks what it means
to 'die for love', point
here.

If someone asks how tall I am, frown
and measure with your fingers the space
between the creases on your forehead.

This tall.

The soul sometimes leaves the body, then returns.
When someone doesn't believe that,
walk back into my house.

Like this.

When lovers moan,
they're telling our story.

Like this.

I am a sky where spirits live.
Stare into this deepening blue,
while the breeze says a secret.

Like this.

When someone asks what there is to do,
light the candle in his hand.

Like this.

How did Joseph's scent come to Jacob?

Huuuuu.

How did Jacob's sight return?

Huuuu.

A little wind cleans the eyes.

Like this.

When Shams comes back from Tabriz,
he'll put just his head around the edge
of the door to surprise us

Like this.

Rumi, rendering by Coleman Barks

Your Turn

Try a poem which switches between time frames using stanza breaks.

—

You're running two films together. Rumi has a series of spiritual and biblical images – the moon and clouds, a sky full of spirits, Jacob's sight returning – running against a slow-mo movie of two people embracing.

—

Your films don't have to be romantic – but the big spiritual images colliding with simple concrete ones works well, as always.

—

Think of an important experience that you have had. It doesn't have to be romantic. Mountain climbing, family moments, time with friends, even a death or loss of love can be just as moving.

Run a little film of it in your head.

Remember everything you have learned about image building, using all the senses, ordering, volta.

Use that capacity to make another little film – of the images you want to connect with your experience.

What moon? What sky? What god?

—

Now, connect the two across stanzas –

—

You can use the Rumi line if you like:

When someone asks you what happiness/friendship/grief/ loss . . . is like

Say, like the time . . .

And when someone asks what it means . . . say

And when someone asks what to do . . .

And when someone asks how you live . . .

—

The magic comes from the two time frames progressively joining up, so try to make sure this happens in your ending, too.

More Practice:
The 'Water' Challenge

If you've taken 'The Blessing' challenge, try one with Robert Lowell's 'Water'. This poem also sounds, like 'The Blessing', artless, but is written in short, tight lines and regular stanzas.

Each line takes us somewhere different in space, each stanza takes us somewhere else in time, and the short spiky stanzas themselves form rocky islands like the islands in the landscape and the islands in the memory of the poet.

To take the 'Water' challenge, copy the poem and remove all the line breaks and stanza breaks. Make a cup of tea, come back to your screen, and, without looking at the original poem, try to put the line breaks and stanza

Water

It was a Maine lobster town—
each morning boatloads of hands
pushed off for granite
quarries on the islands,

and left dozens of bleak
white frame houses stuck
like oyster shells
on a hill of rock,

and below us, the sea lapped
the raw little match-stick
mazes of a weir,
where the fish for bait were trapped.

Remember? We sat on a slab of rock.
From this distance in time
it seems the color
of iris, rotting and turning purpler,

but it was only
the usual gray rock
turning the usual green
when drenched by the sea.

breaks back in. Then
check the original: what
have you lost, and what
have you gained? (N.B. It
is a particularly hard
poem to improve.)

Exercises like this work
well on a computer
screen, because the white
space there is expansive
and slightly vibrant too,
and supremely easy to
manipulate. It's a
wonderful place to focus
on the choices you are
making when you break a
line or a stanza, and to
create habits of looking
for and finding those
breaks. If you keep
puzzling, you will grow
your own process, and
this will help you to sound
like yourself.

The sea drenched the rock
at our feet all day,
and kept tearing away
flake after flake.

One night you dreamed
you were a mermaid clinging to a wharf-pile,
and trying to pull
off the barnacles with your hands.

We wished our two souls
might return like gulls
to the rock. In the end,
the water was too cold for us.

Robert Lowell

The Ring Road:
A Poem with No Stanzas

Perhaps all your time travel is taking you to the point where you can write your own poem. That's what Ocean Vuong thinks. He takes a journey into his childhood, where he is traumatically leaving Vietnam, to speak to his child self. He gives himself some reassurance: mostly, that he will arrive at the point of writing the poem, the point where he will have his own room and the ability to write his experiences, where he can put himself in a line of gay poets (Frank O'Hara, Roger Reeves) and imagine loving his own work and himself.

A poem like this can't have stanza breaks, because there are not gaps in time: everything is

Someday I'll Love Ocean Vuong
(after Frank O'Hara / after Roger Reeves)

Ocean, don't be afraid.
The end of the road is so far ahead
it is already behind us.
Don't worry. Your father is only your father
until one of you forgets. Like how the spine
won't remember its wings
no matter how many times our knees
kiss the pavement. Ocean,
are you listening? The most beautiful part
of your body is wherever
your mother's shadow falls.
Here's the house with childhood
whittled down to a single red trip wire.
Don't worry. Just call it *horizon*
& you'll never reach it.
Here's today. Jump. I promise it's not
a lifeboat. Here's the man
whose arms are wide enough to gather
your leaving. & here the moment,
just after the lights go out, when you can still see
the faint torch between his legs.
How you use it again & again
to find your own hands.
You asked for a second chance
& are given a mouth to empty out of.

wrapping itself around its own self. The lines, too, have to slip easily one into the next.

There's a video of Ocean Vuong reading this poem on the internet which is well worth looking up.

Don't be afraid, the gunfire
is only the sound of people
trying to live a little longer
& failing. Ocean, Ocean –
get up. The most beautiful part of your body
is where it's headed. & remember,
loneliness is still time spent
with the world. Here's
the room with everyone in it.
Your dead friends passing
through you like wind
through a wind chime. Here's a desk
with the gimp leg & a brick
to make it last. Yes, here's a room
so warm & blood-close,
I swear, you will wake—
& mistake these walls
for skin.

Ocean Vuong

Your Turn

For your last bit of time travel, think of a moment in your past when something changed. You're going to give that younger self some advice.

Where is your younger self? Realize her in images, using the Furniture Game and all your image-making skills.

What do you want to tell her?

Where will she end up?

Borrow some of Ocean Vuong's opening phrases as prompts, and write your poem down the page without gaps.

—

Your name . . . don't be afraid . . .

Don't worry . . .

Your father . . .

Here's the house . . .

Jump . . .

I promise . . .

The most beautiful part of your body . . .

& remember . . .

Your dead friends . . .

Yes, here's a room . . .

Are You a Poet Yet?

Conversation with a Poet

Are you a poet?
Yes, I am.
How do you know?
I've written poems.
If you've written poems it means you were a poet.

Miroslav Holub

This book will not have made you a poet if being a poet means being effortlessly gifted, a bard. All poets struggle. Only very rarely does even the most gifted and hard-working poet write a perfect poem in an hour, from inspiration to final draft, and feel happy with it. Being practised, published, praised and prize-winning makes no difference: we all recognize Miroslav Holub's line 'you *were* a poet'; we all sigh as we look at the doggerel we seem to have scribbled on a page and remember the glorious moment of inspiration and insight we intended it to represent.

But I hope this book, and reading lots of poetry, might have helped you to acquire a writing process you can use to attack that messy draft and make it work a bit better, then a bit better again. And, even more importantly, I hope it has given you the sense that you are entitled to do this, that you are allowed to join in the conversation of poetry, even if, like all poets, you fear your words are sometimes halting.

Writing poetry never stops being challenging, and the biggest challenges are always the simplest – confidence and permission. On the other hand, writing never stops being rewarding, and permission, like a writing process, is something you can learn, something you can give yourself.

Opening the Door

If you have written several poems and polished them to the best of your ability and put them in your folder, you probably want – at least a bit – to show them to someone. Not the person you have written them about, maybe, but a skilled reader or writer. Or two. Readers who like poems, who can appreciate what you have done.

Finding such a person or people can be hard, but it's worth a little perseverance. Find out if there is a local writing group and go along, bearing in mind that these groups always have their own dynamics and a variety of members, not all of whom will be sympathetic. Try a writing course – at your local university or college, or a residential one, such as those run by the Arvon Foundation. Groups vary a lot and have different, sometimes gruesome, histories so be careful of yourself. You can't expect to go into a group as a newbie and be the centre of attention. But if you find yourself in a group where hearing and listening are not happening for anyone, have no shame in leaving by the nearest door.

You can also go online. Twitter, Facebook, Instagram et al. are great places to put finished work when you are confident in it – but they are also made of words, just like your poem, and some of those words can be cruel. There is something especially destructive about written criticism of new poems – it's just too easy to believe.

Do you want to send your work out to magazines and publishers? It's a slow, difficult, frustrating process – but one you may feel compelled to join. If so, start reading poetry journals, both online and in print. Send to the ones you admire. Be prepared to wait.

Whether you do or not, it is still worth thinking about your work as a whole. Which poem sits best next to which? If you were putting together a pamphlet or book, which would go first? These aren't hubristic questions – they're part of your creative process. Poems belong together. Assembling a pamphlet is a creative act: word-process your own if you like. Or simply file poems together. What matters is that the poems belong together, and to you.

7
YOUR POEM

Your Poem

I hope, if you have come this far, that you have written some poems and have them sitting around you in notebooks and computer files; that your mind strays to them when you are working; and that when you go home and get them out, you can see little things here and there to make better, things that only you would notice, things that are part of your writing process.

I hope you now think of an image in your mind as something you can capture, a sentence as something you can improve, and a poem as something you can reply to.

As a last thought, here are four poems about poetry. Any of them is a good model.

Choose one and write a poem called 'My Poem': what it tastes of and smells of, what colour and weather it is, and where it is journeying across the great page of time and space.

Introduction to Poetry

I ask them to take a poem
and hold it up to the light
like a colour slide

or press an ear against its hive.

I say drop a mouse into a poem
and watch him probe his way out,

or walk inside the poem's room
and feel the walls for a light switch.

I want them to waterski
across the surface of a poem
waving at the author's name on the shore.

But all they want to do
is tie the poem to a chair with rope
and torture a confession out of it.

They begin beating it with a hose
to find out what it really means.

Billy Collins

Sweetness, Always

Why such harsh machinery?
Why, to write down the stuff
and people of every day,
must poems be dressed up in gold,
or in old and fearful stone?

I want verses of felt or feather
which scarcely weigh, mild verses
with the intimacy of beds
where people have loved and dreamed.
I want poems stained
by hands and everydayness.

Verses of pastry which melt
into milk and sugar in the mouth,
air and water to drink,
the bites and kisses of love.
I long for eatable sonnets,
poems of honey and flour.

Vanity keeps prodding us
to lift ourselves skyward
or to make deep and useless
tunnels underground.
So we forget the joyous
love-needs of our bodies.
We forget about pastries.
We are not feeding the world.

In Madras a long time since,
I saw a sugary pyramid,
a tower of confectionery –
one level after another,
and in the construction, rubies,
and other blushing delights,
medieval and yellow.

Someone dirtied his hands
to cook up so much sweetness.

Brother poets from here
and there, from earth and sky,
from Medellin, from Veracruz,
Abyssinia, Antofagasta,
do you know the recipe for honeycombs?

Let's forget about all that stone.

Let your poetry fill up
the equinoctial pastry shop
our mouths long to devour –
all the children's mouths
and the poor adults' also.
Don't go on without seeing,
relishing, understanding
all these hearts of sugar.

Don't be afraid of sweetness.

With or without us,
sweetness will go on living
and is infinitely alive,
forever being revived,
for it's in a man's mouth,
whether he's eating or singing,
that sweetness has its place

Pablo Neruda

The Poem at Check-in Desk 56

The poem at check-in desk 56
is removing *tweezers, needles, scissors,*
    nail file, corkscrew, Swiss-army knife
    on a chain, a packet of razor blades,
    lighter fluid, then – finally –
    mightier than the sword, *a pen,*
from its word hoard, or vocabulary.

The poem has packed its own baggage.
No one could have interfered with its message.

The poem joins the queue for Departures,
casually drops some further nouns
in a tray, *wallet, keys, change,*
    comb, walkman, mobile phone.
Supposing we laid the poem itself
on the belt, conveyed it into the X-ray:

there, would we see its mystery
on the screen, the poem as living thing?
Or a scatter of commas, a few full stops,
like shrapnel lodged in something spectral?

The poem climbs the steps to the door of the plane
in the wind, and stoops to enter.
A thought crosses the poem's mind:
it could be starring in the film of its life.

The poem reclines, clicks the belt
around its middle verse, fiddles
with the air vent, the reading light,
eyes some lyric passing in the aisle.
The poem unfurls a paper like a sail, shakes

its head at the state of the world, refolds it,
tucks it into the pocket, hums,
drums its fingers on the arm rest.
At take-off, the poem relaxes, closes its eyes.

This poem is in for a pleasant flight.
It's of western dress and appearance, white,
clean-shaven, not in the least suspicious.
It doesn't attract any undue attention,
nor does it hold controversial opinions.

The poem is afraid, these days, and might agree
if it seemed for the best, for the good of the nation,
to sing the anthem with the other citizens,
hand on heart, or hoist a flag
on the lawn each morning, yawning, for a time,
but so far, such measures haven't been required.

We'll leave it now, at its destination,
under the airport's strip-lit glare,
strolling through customs, with nothing to declare.

Colette Bryce

I Want a Poem

I want a poem
with the texture of a colander
on the pastry.

A verse
of pastry so rich
it leaves gleam on your fingertips.

A poem
that stings like the splash of boiling oil
as you drop the pastry in.

A poem
that sits on a silver plate with
nuts and chocolates, served up to guests who
sit cross legged on the thoshak.

A poem
as vibrant as our saffron tea
served up at Eid.

Let your poetry
texture the blank paper
like a prism splitting light.

Don't leave without seeing all the colours.

Shukria Rezaei (eighteen)

List of Poem Titles

Chapter 1 Getting Started

4   'The Table' by Edip Cansever

9   'The Never-Ending Pile' by Michael Egbe

10   'Bin' by Mohamed Assaf

12   'Some People' by Rita Ann Higgins

16   'Things I Learned at University' by Kate Bingham

18   'Things I Learned at Military School' by Michael Egbe

21   'A View of Things' by Edwin Morgan

25   'No Maths Involved' by Han Sun Nkumu

27   'Love's Dog' by Jen Hadfield

Chapter 2 Images

37   'Hope' by Emily Dickinson

38   'Fame' by Emily Dickinson

39   'Want' by Rachel Gittens

40   'Harlem' by Langston Hughes

42   'Hard to Say' by Carol Ann Duffy

45   'Hope' by Linnet Drury

46   'Poem for a Man with No Sense of Smell' by Kate Clanchy

47   'Sometimes your sadness is a yacht' by Jack Underwood

50   'Happiness' by Jane Kenyon

52   'Love Comes Back' by Hera Lindsay Bird

57   'Grief' by Aisha Borja

59   'The Summer Day' by Mary Oliver

63   'It Ain't What You Do, It's What It Does to You' by Simon Armitage

66   'Fountains' by Azfa Awad

69   'Patagonia' by Kate Clanchy

70   'A Guide to Love in Icelandic' by Rebecca Perry

72   'Your Mother and My Mother' by Khwāja Shams-ud-Dīn Muḥammad Ḥāfeẓ-e Shīrāzī (Hafiz)

75   'Brother' by Sana Ul-Hasan

Chapter 3 Building Your Writing Process: Lists, Plots and Turns

83   'Not the Furniture Game' by Simon Armitage

88   'I Want the Confidence of' by Raymond Antrobus

93   'I want the faith' by Linnet Drury

95   'Wasp' by Rebecca Perry

97   'Cow' by Selima Hill

100   'Moon' by Iesha Jennings

101   'Today' by Frank O'Hara

103   'Ode' by Freya Carter

105   'My Heart' by Kim Addonizio

106   'A Birthday' by Christina Rossetti

107   'Ellipse' by Helen Woods

Chapter 4 Summoning Spells: Elegies, Letters, Odes and Things
that Get in the Way

114   'Remember' by Rabindranath Tagore

115   'My Mother Country' by Rukiya Khatun

120   'Jade' by Melissa Lee-Houghton

124   'Lines on Roger Hilton's Watch' by W. S. Graham

129   'Soup Sister' by Rebecca Perry

134   'My Blue Hen' by Ann Gray

136   'Chair' by Sally Davis

Chapter 5 Finding Your Sound

145   'I Come From' by Robert Seatter

147   'I Come From . . .' by Azfa Awad

154   'Animals' by Frank O'Hara

159   'On This Island' by W. H. Auden

160   'Sylhet' by Rukiya Khatun

161   'Look stranger,' by Vivien Urban

165   'If They Should Come for Us' by Fatimah Asghar

Chapter 6 The White Space: Time Travel

175   'The Catch' by Simon Armitage

177   'A Blessing' by James Wright

180   'Time-Travel' by Sharon Olds

184   'Burnt Kabob' by Rumi

187   'A Glass of Tea' by Shukria Rezaei

189 'In That Year' by Kim Moore

192 'My Beast' by Lorraine Mariner

197 'If anyone asks you' by Rumi

202 'Water' by Robert Lowell

204 'Someday I'll Love Ocean Vuong' by Ocean Vuong

207 'Conversation with a Poet' by Miroslav Holub

Chapter 7: Your Poem

215 'Introduction to Poetry' by Billy Collins

216 'Sweetness, Always' by Pablo Neruda

219 'The Poem at Check-In Desk 56' by Colette Bryce

221 'I Want a Poem' by Shukria Rezaei

List of 'Permission to Write' Sections

28   Permission to Write: Join the Conversation

76   Permission to Write: Read Like a Poet

109   Permission to Write: Believe in Your Future and Your Past

139   Permission to Write: Defeating Your Inner Policeman

169   Permission to Write: Sounding Right

207   Permission to Write: Are You a Poet Yet?

List of 'Room to Write' Sections

30   Room to Write: Make Room for Your Poems – and for Yourself

77   Room to Write: Room for Your Poems: Get Hold of Poetry

111   Room to Write: Your Poetry Place, Your Poetry Palace

141   Room to Write: Private Space

171   Room to Write: Listen Out

209   Room to Write: Opening the Door

List of 'In General' Sections

19 In General: Don't Try to Rhyme (right now)

26 In General: If I Borrow a Shape is it Still My Own Poem?

48 In General: First Edits: Make Your Poem Fresher Not Grander

58 In General: Don't Hang Around with the Gerunds (they're just trying to glue up your poem)

62 In General: Titles

68 In General: How Far Can You Go?

87 In General: First Lines: No Time to Clear Your Throat

91 In General: Leaving a Poem to Rise

94 In General: Last Lines: Keep Out of the Pulpit

104 In General: Seeing Your Poem Freshly

108 In General: Are You Stuck but Know that There is More Poem to Write?

119 In General: How True is Your Truth?

123 In General: Sounds that Tell You Something

128 In General: Does Your Poem Want to Be About Something (or Someone) Else?

133 In General: Poems Have Plots

137 In General: The Storyboard Test

151 In General: Finding Your Own Rhythm

157 In General: Where Your Rhythm Breaks

164 In General: Punctuation: Poetry Percussion

179 In General: Edge Words

183 In General: What Track is Your Poem Making?

191 In General: Capital Letters

196 In General: Find a Rule from Inside Your Poem

Acknowledgements

This book is built on poems so I'm grateful to all the poets whose work I've used for sharing that energy; and to Carol Ann Duffy, Simon Armitage, Rebecca Perry, Sally Davis and Raymond Antrobus, in particular, for being so generous with their time and with my real-life students. I'd like to thank the Arvon Foundation, where I learned so much of my craft as a teacher and poet, the Forward Arts Foundation for their constant support over many years, and my colleagues at the University of Reading for their warmth and respect. Thank you to my agent, Zoë Waldie, and my editor at Picador, Kris Doyle, for backing such an odd project, and to the team at Picador who brought it to life.

Permissions Acknowledgements

'The Table' by Edip Cansever, from *Dirty August: Poems by Edip Cansever*, translated by Julia Clare Tillinghast and Richard Tillinghast, translation © Talisman House USA / 'The Never-Ending Pile' by Michael Egbe © Michael Egbe 2020 / 'Bin' by Mohamed Assaf © Mohamed Assaf 2020 / 'Some People' by Rita Ann Higgins, from *Throw in the Vowels: New and Selected Poems*, Bloodaxe Books, 2005 / 'Things I Learned at University' by Kate Bingham, from *Cohabitation*, Seren, 1998 / 'Things I Learned at Military School' by Michael Egbe © Michael Egbe 2020 / 'A View of Things' by Edwin Morgan (*Collected Poems*, 1997) is reprinted here by kind permission of Carcanet Press Limited, Manchester, UK / 'No Maths Involved' by Han Sun Nkumu © Han Sun Nkumu 2020 / 'Love's Dog' by Jen Hadfield, from *Nigh-No-Place*, Bloodaxe Books, 2008 / 'Hope' by Emily Dickinson, from *The Poems of Emily Dickinson: Reading Edition*, edited by Ralph W. Franklin, Cambridge, Mass.: The Belknap Press of Harvard University Press, Copyright © 1998, 1999 by the President and Fellows of Harvard College. Copyright © 1951, 1955, 1979, 1983 by the President and Fellows of Harvard College / 'Fame' by Emily Dickinson from *The Poems of Emily Dickinson: Reading Edition*, edited by Ralph W. Franklin, Cambridge, Mass.: The Belknap Press of Harvard University Press, Copyright © 1998, 1999 by the President and Fellows of Harvard College. Copyright © 1951, 1955, 1979, 1983 by the President and Fellows of Harvard College / 'Want' by Rachel Gittens © Rachel Gittens 2020 / 'Harlem' from *The Collected Works of Langston Hughes*, copyright © 2002 by Langston Hughes, reprinted by permission of Harold Ober Associates, Inc. and Serpent's Tail / 'Hard to Say' by Carol Ann Duffy, from *Collected Poems*, Picador, 2015 / 'Hope' by Linnet Drury

Barks, from HarperSanFrancisco, 1995 / 'Water' by Robert Lowell, from *New Selected Poems*, Faber and Faber Ltd, 2017 / 'Someday I'll Love Ocean Vuong' by Ocean Vuong, from *Night Sky With Exit Wounds*, Jonathan Cape, 2017 / 'Conversation with a Poet' by Miroslav Holub, from *Poems Before & After: Collected English Translations*, translated by Ian & Jarmila Milner, Bloodaxe Books, 2006 / 'Introduction to Poetry' by Billy Collins, from *The Apple that Astonished Paris*, University of Arkansas Press, 1988 / 'Sweetness, Always' by Pablo Neruda, translated by Alastair Reid, from *Extravagaria*, Farrar, Straus and Giroux, 1975 / 'The Poem at Check-In Desk 56' by Colette Bryce © Colette Bryce 2004 / 'I Want a Poem' by Shukria Rezaei, from *England: Poems from a School*, Picador, 2018.